MISTAKES
NEW 7-12TH GRADE
TEACHERS
MAKE AND HOW TO PREVENT THEM

Insider Secrets to Avoid Classroom Blunders

KIMBERLY SARMIENTO

199 Mistakes New 7-12th Grade Teachers Make and How to Prevent Them: Insider Secrets to Avoid Classroom Blunders

Copyright © 2017 by Atlantic Publishing Group, Inc.
1405 SW 6th Ave. • Ocala, Florida 34471 • 800-814-1132 • 352-622-1875–Fax
Web site: www.atlantic-pub.com • E-mail: sales@atlantic-pub.com
SAN Number: 268-1250

No part of this publication may be reproduced, stored in a retrieval system, or transmitted in any form or by any means, electronic, mechanical, photocopying, recording, scanning, or otherwise, except as permitted under Section 107 or 108 of the 1976 United States Copyright Act, without the prior written permission of the Publisher. Requests to the Publisher for permission should be sent to Atlantic Publishing Group, Inc., 1405 SW 6th Ave., Ocala, Florida 34471.

Library of Congress Cataloging-in-Publication Data

Sarmiento, Kimberly, 1975-
   199 mistakes new 7th-12th grade teachers make and how to prevent them : insider secrets to avoid classroom blunders / by Kimberly Sarmiento.
      pages cm
   Includes bibliographical references and index.
   ISBN 978-1-60138-964-0 (alk. paper) -- ISBN 1-60138-964-7 (alk. paper) 1. Middle school teaching. 2. High school teaching. 3. First year teachers. I. Title. II. Title: One hundred ninety-nine mistakes new Seventh-Twelfth grade teachers make and how to prevent them.
   LB1623.5.S28 2015
   373.1102--dc23
                                                   2015006558

LIMIT OF LIABILITY/DISCLAIMER OF WARRANTY: The publisher and the author make no representations or warranties with respect to the accuracy or completeness of the contents of this work and specifically disclaim all warranties, including without limitation warranties of fitness for a particular purpose. No warranty may be created or extended by sales or promotional materials. The advice and strategies contained herein may not be suitable for every situation. This work is sold with the understanding that the publisher is not engaged in rendering legal, accounting, or other professional services. If professional assistance is required, the services of a competent professional should be sought. Neither the publisher nor the author shall be liable for damages arising herefrom. The fact that an organization or Web site is referred to in this work as a citation and/or a potential source of further information does not mean that the author or the publisher endorses the information the organization or Web site may provide or recommendations it may make. Further, readers should be aware that Internet Web sites listed in this work may have changed or disappeared between when this work was written and when it is read.

TRADEMARK: All trademarks, trade names, or logos mentioned or used are the property of their respective owners and are used only to directly describe the products being provided. Every effort has been made to properly capitalize, punctuate, identify and attribute trademarks and trade names to their respective owners, including the use of ® and ™ wherever possible and practical. Atlantic Publishing Group, Inc. is not a partner, affiliate, or licensee with the holders of said trademarks.

Printed in the United States
BOOK PRODUCTION DESIGN: T.L. Price • design@tlpricefreelance.com

Reduce. Reuse. RECYCLE.

A decade ago, Atlantic Publishing signed the Green Press Initiative. These guidelines promote environmentally friendly practices, such as using recycled stock and vegetable-based inks, avoiding waste, choosing energy-efficient resources, and promoting a no-pulping policy. We now use 100-percent recycled stock on all our books. The results: in one year, switching to post-consumer recycled stock saved 24 mature trees, 5,000 gallons of water, the equivalent of the total energy used for one home in a year, and the equivalent of the greenhouse gases from one car driven for a year.

Over the years, we have adopted a number of dogs from rescues and shelters. First there was Bear and after he passed, Ginger and Scout. Now, we have Kira, another rescue. They have brought immense joy and love not just into our lives, but into the lives of all who met them.

We want you to know a portion of the profits of this book will be donated in Bear, Ginger and Scout's memory to local animal shelters, parks, conservation organizations, and other individuals and nonprofit organizations in need of assistance.

– **Douglas & Sherri Brown,**
President & Vice-President of Atlantic Publishing

TABLE OF CONTENTS

Introduction 17

PART ONE: CLASSROOM MANAGEMENT & DISCIPLINE   23

Chapter 1: Leadership Strategies for Teachers 25

Management Style *26*

MISTAKE 1: Letting students direct your class… 27

MISTAKE 2: Not setting goals for your students… 28

The Importance of Professionalism *29*

MISTAKE 3: Letting students call you by your first name… 30

MISTAKE 4: Not being mindful of your appearance… 31

MISTAKE 5: Using contemporary slang… 32

MISTAKE 6: Fraternizing with students… 33

Chapter 2: Planning & Preparation 35

MISTAKE 7: Making the first day all about "fun"… 36

MISTAKE 8: Not defining policies for classroom conduct… 37

MISTAKE 9: Not telling students your academic policies on the first day of school… 38

MISTAKE 10: Not reviewing the student handbook with your students (at least the highlights)… 39

MISTAKE 11: Not working a child's needs into your seating arrangements... 39

MISTAKE 12: Not making the most of student orientation... 40

MISTAKE 13: Not anticipating extra students in your class the first day of school... 42

MISTAKE 14: Not knowing if one of your students have special needs... 42

MISTAKE 15: Not evaluating your students' strengths and weaknesses... 43

MISTAKE 16: Not reviewing previous year's material... 44

MISTAKE 17: Not keeping things simple... 44

Chapter 3: Fairness & Consistency ... 45

MISTAKE 18: Letting "gifted" children direct the class... 48

MISTAKE 19: Letting "big" personalities overshadow you... 50

MISTAKE 20: Making a student feel "small" in order to put them in their place... 51

MISTAKE 21: Being too hard on kids who talk too much... 52

MISTAKE 22: Mixing it up with the class clown... 53

MISTAKE 23: Responding harshly to a disrespectful student... 54

MISTAKE 24: Overcompensating for your perceived shortcomings... 55

MISTAKE 25: Letting bathroom breaks get out of hand... 57

Avoiding Inconsistencies ... 58

MISTAKE 26: Being relaxed one day and firm the next. 59

MISTAKE 27: Showing favoritism... 60

MISTAKE 28: Showing dislike for a student... 62

MISTAKE 29: Using sarcasm... 63

Chapter 4: Discipline Strategies ... 65

Ways Not to Discipline — Ever ... 66

MISTAKE 30: Using ridicule to get a student in line... 66

MISTAKE 31: Cursing… 70

MISTAKE 32: Yelling… 71

MISTAKE 33: Getting physical… 72

Small-Time Discipline Measures **73**

MISTAKE 34: Sending students to the office over small matters… 74

MISTAKE 35: Not knowing your school's unexcused tardy/absence policy… 76

MISTAKE 36: Using classroom control measures that could cause more disruption… 77

Punishment That Might Create Resentment **77**

MISTAKE 37: Using group punishment… 78

MISTAKE 38: Assigning extra work as punishment… 79

MISTAKE 39: Forgetting to reward good behavior… 81

Chapter 5: Managing Distractions 83

Best Friends Forever and Worst Enemies **84**

MISTAKE 40: Letting popularity matter in the classroom… 85

MISTAKE 41: Permitting "innocent" teasing… 86

MISTAKE 42: Letting fights or bickering impact the classroom… 88

MISTAKE 43: Trying to settle a student squabble or restore a broken friendship… 89

MISTAKE 44: Taking sides… 90

MISTAKE 45: Not recognizing and stopping bullying… 90

High-Tech Distractions **91**

MISTAKE 46: Allowing phones and other devices in your classroom… 92

MISTAKE 47: Not confiscating items you do not allow in your classroom… 93

MISTAKE 48: Not making your policy clear to parents and asking for their help in enforcing your rules… 94

MISTAKE 49: Not knowing what to do when a fight erupts… 95

MISTAKE 50: Not dealing with a student's vomiting in a professional manner... 96

MISTAKE 51: Not knowing exactly what to do in case of a fire drill, bomb threats, etc... 96

Boredom *97*

MISTAKE 52: Assigning too much work... 98

MISTAKE 53: Not using hands-on work... 99

MISTAKE 54: Just having your students sit quietly and read their textbook... 100

MISTAKE 55: Not having a back-up plan for interruptions... 101

Chapter 6: Overcoming Challenges to Learning............ 103

MISTAKE 56: Not knowing how to deal with students who have no motivation... 103

MISTAKE 57: Not knowing how to deal with students who have a busy schedule... 105

MISTAKE 58: Not knowing how to deal with students who are not tech-savvy... 106

MISTAKE 59: Not knowing how to deal with students who cannot handle criticism... 107

Chapter 7: Teaching Children Through Puberty 111

MISTAKE 60: Not understanding that girl's periods can come without warning... 112

MISTAKE 61: Commenting on changes the students are experiencing... 113

MISTAKE 62: Permitting sexual harassment... 113

MISTAKE 63: Flirting with students... 114

PART TWO: RELATIONSHIPS   115

Chapter 8: Curriculum Strategies 117

MISTAKE 64: Teaching just so students do well on standardized tests... 118

MISTAKE 65: Teaching as if tests do not matter... 120

MISTAKE 66: Being too hard on children who do not test well in this environment... 121

MISTAKE 67: Getting frustrated with students who are not grasping the material and are not ready to "move on"... 122

MISTAKE 68: Ignoring bad or bored students... 123

MISTAKE 69: Not engaging students who are more advanced... 124

MISTAKE 70: Not recognizing when a student needs to be challenged more... 125

MISTAKE 71: Using words or language your students do not understand... 126

Chapter 9: Teaching Facts, Skills, & Concepts 127

MISTAKE 72: Being opposed to re-teaching facts or concepts students should already know... 129

MISTAKE 73: Not reviewing after shorter school breaks... 131

MISTAKE 74: Expecting transfer students to be on the same page as your class... 132

MISTAKE 75: Thinking a student is slow because they are lacking a certain skill set... 133

MISTAKE 76: Grouping students according to ability... 134

Chapter 10: Tests & Homework 135

The Great Homework Debate 136

MISTAKE 77: Giving "busy work"... 137

MISTAKE 78: Giving too much homework... 139

MISTAKE 79: Not allowing more than one day to complete homework... 140

MISTAKE 80: Assigning homework that is too hard for the students to do alone... 141

MISTAKE 81: Assigning tests or homework without paying attention to the school schedule... 142

Fair Testing ... 143

MISTAKE 82: Only giving tests that leverage one way of learning... 144

MISTAKE 83: Not using a "curve"... 145

MISTAKE 84: Creating overly complex tests... 147

MISTAKE 85: Not allowing enough time for students to complete a test... 148

Identifying & Dealing with Cheating ... 148

MISTAKE 86: Punishing the wrong student for cheating... 149

MISTAKE 87: Letting one student do everything on "group" assignments... 151

MISTAKE 88: Handling plagiarism... 153

Chapter 11: Projects & Reports ... 155

MISTAKE 89: Getting overly creative with book reports... 156

MISTAKE 90: Assigning "art" projects for core subjects... 157

MISTAKE 91: Expecting parents will not be doing at least half the work... 158

MISTAKE 92: Assigning science projects that are just reports... 160

Chapter 12: Student Nightmares ... 161

MISTAKE 93: Calling on students at random to answer questions... 162

MISTAKE 94: Forcing children to do board work... 163

MISTAKE 95: Making children share something about themselves... 164

Chapter 13: Subject-Specific Guidelines 165

MISTAKE 96: Not requiring students to show their work on math tests... 165

MISTAKE 97: Making students read out loud to the class... 166

MISTAKE 98: Overemphasizing date memorization in history........167

MISTAKE 99: Not teaching students proper safety measures in science... 167

MISTAKE 100: Not testing students on spelling rules... 168

MISTAKE 101: Not working with students on their handwriting... 168

Chapter 14: Grading 169

MISTAKE 102: Not grading participation... 170

MISTAKE 103: Grading for neatness... 171

MISTAKE 104: Not grading for neatness... 172

MISTAKE 105: Not giving extra credit... 173

MISTAKE 106: Not giving all of your students the chance to do extra credit... 174

MISTAKE 107: Not offering before or after school help... 174

MISTAKE 108: Not leveraging what the student is good in to help them with their weak areas... 176

MISTAKE 109: Not calling the parents soon enough... 177

MISTAKE 110: Not giving the student the grade he or she earned......179

MISTAKE 111: Being unwilling to fail a student... 180

MISTAKE 112: Not keeping track of grades well... 181

MISTAKE 113: Emphasizing that grades are everything... 182

PART THREE: WHAT YOU TEACH & HOW YOU TEACH IT   183

Chapter 15: Classroom Dictator or Mr./Ms. Softie? *Does being liked matter?*... *185*

MISTAKE 114: Wanting to be everyone's favorite teacher... 186

MISTAKE 115: Responding emotionally to a personal attack... 187

MISTAKE 116: Not staying professional when a student is crying... ..188

MISTAKE 117: Letting a classroom get out of hand while having fun... 191

MISTAKE 118: Being unwilling to explain yourself... 191

MISTAKE 119: Not admitting if you are wrong... 192

MISTAKE 120: Being too relaxed... 193

Chapter 16: Relating to Students that are Different from You 195

MISTAKE 121: Continuing the extrovert vs. introvert "war"... 196

MISTAKE 122: Not being able to communicate with different personalities... 197

MISTAKE 123: Trying to impose your political beliefs on your students... 198

Chapter 17: Recognizing Outside Influence on School Work 201

MISTAKE 124: Assuming a student has a learning disability if they do not... 201

MISTAKE 125: Not tailoring work for a child with a physical or learning disability... 203

MISTAKE 126: Dealing with a physical or learning disability inappropriately... 204

MISTAKE 127: Ignoring a sudden drop in grades... 206

Teens with difficult personal lives 208

MISTAKE 128: Favoring one parent over the other during a divorce... 208

MISTAKE 129: Not being flexible if the student has stress at home... 210

MISTAKE 130: Basing a student's grades on things they have no control over... 211

MISTAKE 131: Promising silence if a student confides in you... 212

MISTAKE 132: Not seeking help from the school counselor... 213

Chapter 18: Relating to Parents/Guardians............... 215

Communicating with parents regarding grades and student progress.. 216

MISTAKE 133: Not communicating with parents in writing... 216

MISTAKE 134: Not sending work/tests home regularly... 217

MISTAKE 135: Letting parents call the shots... 217

MISTAKE 136: Not reporting behavioral issues... 218

MISTAKE 137: Not scheduling parent-teacher conferences... 218

MISTAKE 138: Waiting too long to tell parents you think there is a learning problem... 219

MISTAKE 139: Blaming parents for not supporting a student at home... 220

MISTAKE 140: Blaming the parents if a student is badly behaved at school... 221

MISTAKE 141: Not clearly communicating what the student can do to improve... 222

MISTAKE 142: Not telling the parents if you think the student might have a learning disability... 223

MISTAKE 143: Letting your personal opinion of a parent show... 225

How to deal with divorced parents.. 226

MISTAKE 144: Communicating with one parent, but not the other..... 227

MISTAKE 145: Appearing to favor one parent over the other... 228

MISTAKE 146: Being unwilling to communicate with a step-parent... 229

Teaching Family.. 230

MISTAKE 147: Not making administration aware of the relationship... 230

MISTAKE 148: Letting the child call you by a name the other students cannot use... 230

MISTAKE 149: Working too hard not to show favoritism... 231

Chapter 19: Relating to Other Teachers 233

MISTAKE 150: Not asking for guidance if you need it... 233

MISTAKE 151: Getting involved in campus politics... 234

MISTAKE 152: Getting caught up in gossip... 235

MISTAKE 153: Passing along a false allegation... 236

Chapter 20: Teaching in a Politically-Correct World 237

MISTAKE 154: Letting your religion show... 238

MISTAKE 155: Only celebrating "common" holidays... 239

MISTAKE 156: Letting stereotypes show up in your classroom... 239

MISTAKE 157: Treating girls and boys differently... 240

MISTAKE 158: Not protecting students who may be gay... 241

MISTAKE 159: Allowing students to make fun of a child's accent or culture... 242

MISTAKE 160: Assuming a student needs extra help if they are from another country/culture... 243

MISTAKE 161: Not helping children who live in poverty keep up with the class... 244

PART FOUR: PROFESSIONAL MISTAKES TO AVOID   245

Chapter 21: Choosing Your School Environment 247

MISTAKE 162: Not understanding how different types of "public" schools work... 247

MISTAKE 163: Not understanding the requirements of various "private" schools... 248

Chapter 22: Behavioral Mistakes 251

MISTAKE 164: Using language not fit for children to hear... 251

MISTAKE 165: Showing prejudice or bias... 252

MISTAKE 166: Not being smart about your social media... 253

MISTAKE 167: Dressing inappropriately... 253
MISTAKE 168: Dating someone on the staff... 254
MISTAKE 169: Dating a parent... 255
MISTAKE 170: Not reporting illegal behavior... 256

Chapter 23: Continuous Improvement 257

MISTAKE 171: Not working on your classroom presentation skills... 257
MISTAKE 172: Not planning ahead... 258
MISTAKE 173: Not adjusting your lesson plan if needed... 258
MISTAKE 174: Not adjusting your teaching methods if they appear ineffective... 259
MISTAKE 175: Not reviewing what types of questions your students are struggling with... 259

Chapter 24: Avoiding a Lawsuit 261

MISTAKE 176: Not knowing applicable laws for schools in your county/state... 262
MISTAKE 177: Not making students aware of risks, even ones you think they should know... 262
MISTAKE 178: Not monitoring your students closely while they are in your care... 263
MISTAKE 179: Purposively embarrassing a student... 263
MISTAKE 180: Not removing a student who proves dangerous to another student... 264
MISTAKE 181: Not protecting a student's privacy... 264
MISTAKE 182: Not complying with laws regarding suspicion you must report... 265
MISTAKE 183: Not knowing your student's medical needs... 265
MISTAKE 184: Not documenting communications with parents... 266
MISTAKE 185: Using a student's image without their parents' permission... 266
MISTAKE 186: Dating a student or former student... 267

MISTAKE 187: Drinking or smoking at school... 268

MISTAKE 188: Showing physical displays of affection with students or a teacher... 269

Chapter 25: Impressing Office Staff/Your Boss 271

MISTAKE 189: Avoiding extra work... 271

MISTAKE 190: Not being considerate when using copiers and office equipment... 272

MISTAKE 191: Being overly defensive if a parent or student complains about you... 273

MISTAKE 192: Taking too many sick days... 273

MISTAKE 193: Going over someone's head... 274

MISTAKE 194: Complaining about the classes you are assigned to teach... 274

Chapter 26: Final Thoughts.. 275

MISTAKE 195: Not smiling... 275

MISTAKE 196: Not praising a job well done... 276

MISTAKE 197: Not being warm and friendly... 276

MISTAKE 198: Not making friends among your coworkers... 277

MISTAKE 199: Not having any fun... 277

Bibliography 279

Contributors 281

Index 283

Author Biography 287

INTRODUCTION

"The mediocre teacher tells, the good teacher explains, the superior teacher demonstrates, and the great teacher inspires," said William A. Ward. A poet, inspirational writer, and man of great faith, Ward points out what separated the type of teachers people remember and loved from those who did not inspire them in the classroom.

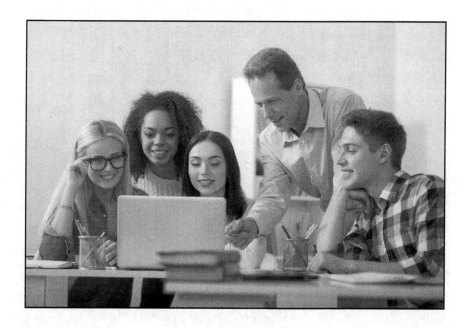

My friend recently posted a "throwback Thursday" picture of her and her father from our high school days. Since he has been deceased for a few years, she naturally received wonderful comments. While he was a great father to her — and to many of us, as well — he was also one of the greatest teachers I ever had.

Our families had been friends for several years, so I respected him in and out of the classroom. I believe he was a great teacher, but I might have been biased. It always warms my heart when I read posts about how he was such a great teacher and inspired his students to love math and science. Students did not just love him because he was a fun teacher — he taught them two of the most difficult subjects you could imagine in high school — physics and calculus. They loved him because he made learning fun, and he earned the respect of hundreds of students along the way.

Having a legacy such as his motivates many individuals to enter the field of teaching. From your first year to your retirement, where hundreds of students praise the impact you had on them, the journey is a long one. Furthermore, the classroom is a different world than even the one you learned in. Technology, standardized tests, parents, and even students are different. Some of the challenges you face will be different than your predecessors, yet some will be very much the same.

As a first-year teacher, whether or not you are able to inspire your students will likely be determined by a combination of your personality and passion as well as a strategic effort to avoid common teaching mistakes. This book cannot help you bring things to your classroom that are not intrinsic in you, but it is dedicated to help you learn from dozens of seasoned teachers who once stood in your shoes.

The first thing you must understand about teaching is that it should be a calling, not just a profession. You have probably heard the saying "Love what you do and never work a day in your life." My advice, that teaching should be a calling not just a job, is not about any relatively false philosophy such as this. I love being a writer. My work spans several different genres, such as journalism, business, academic, technical and career development, and yet, I can assure you that there are days when my job is difficult.

Having first-hand teaching experience (on the collegiate level) and interviewing dozens of elementary school teachers, there will be days when it feels like the hardest and most unappreciated profession around, no matter how much you love teaching (nurses will, of course, vie for this title, but I believe it is a tight contest). "It is long hours and hard work, but it is all for the benefit of the students," says Sara Razaire of Volusia County Schools.

As a teacher, people will look at you as if your job is not ***that*** hard. You will hear comments about how you have more time off than other professions (an entire summer to kick back and relax!), and they will often assume your day ends when the school day ends.

Other teachers, like Shay Matthews, former teacher of Tavares Christian School, say, "If you do not go home exhausted and spent, then you did not do your job." But those not in the know may fail to take into consideration the amount of time you spend grading papers at home or preparing for future classroom assignments. Many people will also never realize that you will spend your personal dollars on school supplies. You might even notice numerous people making online comments about unreasonable demands by teachers for greater pay or benefits.

In addition to the general public, and perhaps even your friends failing to understand how hard your job is, how much time you spend at it, and how little money you really make at it (particularly early on), many parents will somehow forget just how difficult little Johnny or Sally is to manage at home. Despite the fact that parents will jokingly lament how their jobs grow exponentially harder with each additional child they have, even they can fail to understand how challenging it is to manage a classroom of 20+ students. You cannot necessarily expect buckets of sympathy from your student's parents; your job will be difficult, and it might even be thankless. Many people will not value or respect your work. You might even have to live with people questioning your intelligence, qualifications, and merit as a teacher. Have you heard the delightful saying, "Those who can, do; those who cannot, teach"? You will have to live with all of this as well as excel in your classroom to succeed. This is not the recipe for a job someone gets because they cannot figure out what else to do. **This is the formula for a calling.**

If you are called, then this book is dedicated to making your initial foray into the profession of teaching with as much ease as possible. As the title denotes, this researched guide compiles 199 mistakes you should avoid as a new middle school or high school teacher. Some of these mistakes might seem obvious, whereas others may be actions and attitudes you have not even considered. This book contains humorous antidotes, stories from dozens of established teachers, and practical advice to help you succeed on the first day of school.

The book is broken down into four parts: **Classroom Management & Discipline Mistakes to Avoid**, **Teaching Mistakes to Avoid**, **Relationship Mistakes to Avoid**, and **Professional Mistakes to Avoid**.

The first section — Classroom Management & Discipline Mistakes to Avoid — deals with a wide range of issues related to managing your classroom, avoiding distractions, and employing discipline in a professional manner.

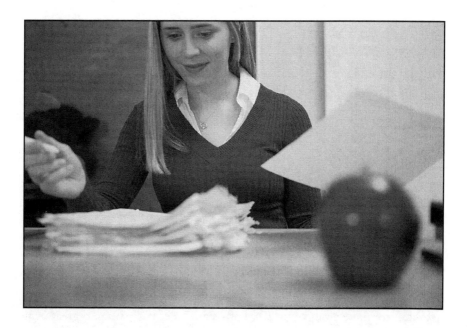

The second section — Teaching Mistakes to Avoid — addresses issues related to curriculum development, teaching, testing, and grading. While this is the subject area you probably spent the most time on while earning your degree, I have still compiled a list of advice from both teachers and professionals that should prove beneficial as you put what you have learned into practice.

The third section — Relationship Mistakes to Avoid — is not about your dating or married life. As much as I argued that teaching must be a calling, I also want to emphasize how important relationships are in regards to your teaching experience. Your job will be much more than communicating information to eager sponges waiting to learn. The relationships you form with students, parents, and even colleagues will define your teaching career — for better or worse. Therefore, the second section will guide you in building good relationships and avoiding pitfalls that come from having "bad people skills." This section will also offer some solid guidance on how to deal with bad relationships. No matter how much of a great teacher you are, not every student or parent is going to love you. Knowing how to deal, or at least how not to deal, with those who do not like you or feel that you are not doing your job will help you succeed in your job even during the hardest moments.

The last section — Professional Mistakes to Avoid — focuses on your professional development and how to avoid issues that will delay your career advancement. I would love to tell you that if you excel in teaching your students and managing your relationships well, then that will be enough to have a great career as a teacher. Just like professionals all around the country have to deal with politics, you will have to navigate through school politics. You will also have professional standards you need to meet, professional development you will need to complete, and career decisions to make along your 20 to 30-year career path. Since a great deal of my professional life is spent working with people who are seeking new employment and/or career advancement, this book includes important information to cover for new teachers. Therefore, the last portion of this book is dedicated to sharing stories from established teachers on how to gain tenure and stay employed in a world of budget cuts, restricted resources, and standards.

This book will help prepare you mentally for the issues you could face and develop strategies to overcome or at least bypass each of these 199 mistakes. If you must first learn in order to teach, I encourage you to learn from the mistakes of others shared in these pages and enjoy your first days of teaching even more by avoiding these stumbling blocks to success.

PART ONE

CLASSROOM MANAGEMENT & DISCIPLINE

After completing your bachelor's degree, several teaching practicum programs, and required state certifications, you send your résumé to multiple schools with great zeal. After several interviews with multiple principals, you receive an offer to teach at a wonderful school and prepare yourself for the beginning of your teaching journey.

As excited as you are to start your teaching career, you are likely full of questions and concerns, which led you to this book. There are many, much more than 199, mistakes you can make in your first year of teaching and throughout your career. Some you should simply accept and learn from since they will make you a better teacher. Others you will want to avoid altogether.

The first section of this book is a compilation of "do nots" and "should nots" that will hopefully make the experience of managing a classroom easier for you. In a book written for new teachers, it might make a lot of sense to begin with the subject of teaching. However, you know you will be teaching, and while I will cover that subject in this book, you have likely been instructed on it a great deal while you were earning your degree.

What you might not be fully aware of is how much you need to take and maintain "command" of your classroom. Therefore, the very first mistake you should avoid is…***Not thinking of yourself as a manager or leader.*** I have seen some fabulous teachers at work and while many of them did not belong leading a team in corporate America, they all held control over their classrooms. I believe this is necessary to your success as a teacher, so this section is dedicated to answering questions you might have on student management and discipline.

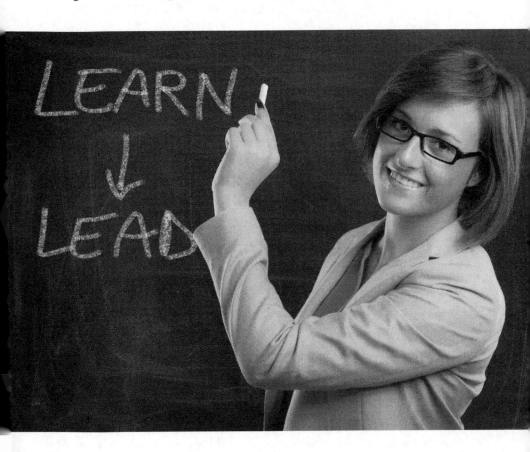

CHAPTER 1
Leadership Strategies for Teachers

You may not consider yourself a natural born leader and you might have little to no desire to advance into administration. Perhaps you went into teaching because all you wanted to do was educate — not lead. What is the old saying? "Those who can, do. Those who can't, teach."

No line of thinking could be further from the truth when addressing the subject of teaching middle and high school students of today. Perhaps it was never correct. While some of your students will naturally give you respect, others will make you earn it. To do so, you must find within you the ability to stand in front of your students and command their attention.

I was in my late 20's when I worked as an adjunct professor for a mid-sized university in Oklahoma located near a military base. As a result, I found myself not just teaching 18-22 year-olds, but also men and women who had been working on their degrees for more than a decade. At least half of my students were older than me and I was, on more than one occasion, confused for a fellow student on the first day of class. Yet, I was still their teacher, and I had to make them believe I deserved both their respect and their recognition as an expert in my field.

As a first year teacher, assuming you followed a traditional route through college, you could be as little as four or five years older than your students.

That does not mean they will not respect you, but you should take care to avoid mistakes that could undermine your authority and make managing your classroom harder than it needs to be. This chapter is dedicated to helping you recognize and bypass those errors.

Management Style

There are many different types of leaders in the world. In fact, ask a room full of people to name a great leader, and you hear the names of government officials, military generals, corporate executives, and even sports icons. They may have little in common except that they all led a group of people to achieve something that brought them recognition in the process.

How they led can vary dramatically, from an autocratic style where the manager makes decisions unilaterally to democratic leaders who empower their followers to make decisions by majority. While you might feel uncomfortable thinking of yourself as an autocrat, I am sure you can see that leading by vote would be a poor idea in your classroom.

As you decide what leadership tools and techniques you feel comfortable employing in your classroom, consider the following advice:

MISTAKE 1

Letting students direct your class...

You do not need to be oppressive or militaristic, but you do need to manage the activity of the classroom. You need to be the one that controls the lecture, discussion, and pace at which you cover the material. Doing this successfully will require planning, analysis, resourcefulness, and flexibility. For you to meet the needs of your students, cover the required curriculum, and ensure you are seen as the leader of your class, you need to plan ahead while monitoring the performance of your class to identify needed adjustments.

It is acceptable for a student to ask a question that leads the class off on an educational tangent every now and then, but you need to recognize when to bring the class back to the original topic. You can achieve this by making sure the tangent subject ties in with the material you need to cover or simply by tabling the discussion to a later date and returning to the original material.

In order to ensure that your students are not leading you off topic too often, measure your progress against your lesson plans. If you find that you are not covering your planned curriculum on a regular basis, you might need to make sure you — not your students — are setting the tone for your class.

MISTAKE 2

Not setting goals for your students…

"Before you are a leader, success is all about growing yourself. When you become a leader, success is all about growing others," said Jack Welch, former CEO of General Electric. Welch grew GE into Fortune 500 Company and mentored countless future business leaders along the way.

I do not know what potential your students hold within them, but I do know that you should set goals for their development that extend beyond scoring well on a standardized test. Giving your students an objective — be it individual or group — is beneficial on multiple levels. Having a goal helps engage students on a higher level and establishes you as their leader to guide them in achieving their objectives.

A goal for your students could be to challenge each of them to improve their graded performance a certain percentage from one grading period to the next. It could also be to challenge each class to read more biographies than other classes for that school year. I believe it is especially helpful to give students who struggle in your subject matter goals for improvement. If you can train the student to focus on improvement rather than just their letter grade, you can help them fulfill their potential — whatever that might be.

The Importance of Professionalism

Remember that the closer you are to your students in age, the more you will need to use an aura of professionalism to distinguish yourself as their teacher, not their peer. Assuming you are a new graduate, you may not have spent a great deal of time in a corporate environment. That being the case, you might not yet realize how important it is to dress, speak, and present yourself in a professional manner. You might not even know what that means.

Professionalism for teachers means remembering that you are the leader of the classroom and you are *not* your students' friend. You, or one of your friends, might have had a tattoo, piercings, or oddly dyed hair in college. Now that you are professional, you might be expected to remove, change, or cover up things that were once considered expressions of your personality.

It might seem unfair that this is expected of you, but remember that perception often becomes reality. If you are perceived by students, parents, or administration as unprofessional or as a "bad fit" for the corporate culture that has developed at the school/district at which you work, you may not keep your job. I will delve into this concept at greater lengths later in the book, but for now, just consider the importance of professionalism in establishing yourself as the leader of your classroom.

MISTAKE 3

Letting students call you by your first name...

While it is probably not a good idea for any middle or high school teacher to allow their students to call them by their first name, it is even less wise if you are young. In the U.S., we are not as formal as other cultures in this regard, but there is an unspoken rule that addressing someone by their first name denotes a level of familiarity that should not be present between you and your students.

Thinking back to how you addressed adults as a child, your teachers, or even your college professors, it is likely that there was a difference in how you were allowed to address those in some position of authority over you versus how you addressed your friends. If you believe your students would benefit from a more relaxed learning environment, pay attention to how your colleagues are addressed by their students, and try to imagine if your approach will earn you the respect of other teachers. If the answer is no, adjust your strategy accordingly.

MISTAKE 4
Not being mindful of your appearance...

Having worked with dozens of career coaches, I can promise you that appearance matters in interviews. In fact, given how little a hiring manager can really learn about you in an interview, appearance and how you present yourself might be the leading factor in whether or not you are hired.

"Seeing is believing" is an idiom that dates back hundreds of years. The idea is that tangible proof is necessary for belief or trust. However, we have come to think of it as also meaning that people will believe what they see. Therefore, no matter how much we rage against the shallowness of being judged merely on our looks, the simple truth is that appearance matters.

Being mindful of your appearance does not just mean being clean and well put together; it also means presenting the correct image to those around you. The good news is that you do not need to look like an airbrushed movie star on the cover of a magazine to ensure your continued employment. However, dressing (and looking) like your students expect adults to dress (and look) is an important consideration when seeking to establish yourself as the authority in your classroom.

To this day, two of my high school teachers stand out in my memory for their appearance. One looked like she came straight out of the movie *Grease 2* with tight sweaters stretched over an ample bosom and big, bleached blonde hair. The other teacher was an older woman who was eccentric in her taste to say the least. In these instances, being unusual did not cost a teacher respect, but being overly sensual did. It might be unfair, but it is reality.

As you establish yourself as the leader of your classroom, make sure you look the part. If you are unsure what is acceptable and what is not, turn again to your colleagues and use them as your guide. Make sure you understand the school dress code for students, and govern yourself accordingly — you will do yourself no favors by wearing something that would get a student sent home.

MISTAKE 5
Using contemporary slang…

As a writer who was born in the 1970s, I learned to use email, text, and social media as an adult. Ergo, I am mostly in the dark when it comes to the abbreviated slang that is quickly turning into another language among the tech-savvy generation that followed mine. Of course, my love for words and grammar causes me to suffer great pain when others slaughter the English language around me.

So having fully admitted my bias, I am still going to advise you to stay away from slang when you lecture your students. Use of the occasional phrase to emphasize a point is acceptable, but one of the greatest ways you can establish your qualifications to instruct your students to your class is to simply "sound" smart. You do not do so through frequent use of slang, vulgarity, or "text speak."

I realize that every generation has words that seep into their vernacular so extensively that they no longer recognize the words as being slang. Be careful to do this as little as possible if for no other reason than to set a good example for your students. After all, you can hardly expect them to speak or write any better than you do in your lectures. Whatever standard you have for your students, set it higher for yourself.

MISTAKE 6

Fraternizing with students...

In college, when students and professors are all adults, the lines of fraternization can blur. In middle and high school, you need to create and maintain strong boundaries for socialization with your students. When you are old enough to have a child the same age as your students, you might have to alternate between the role of parent and teacher, but until that is the case, you should strive to be seen as your student's teacher in and out of the classroom.

If you attend the same church as some of your students or somehow see your students in some other social setting, do not relax their perception and tell them to call you "Jim." If you see your students at a sports outing, parade, concert, or other community event, treat them as if they are your student, and maintain your professionalism around them.

While it is understandable that you will want to relax and just "be yourself" when you leave your classroom, you should be mindful of the fact that when you attend school functions or events where a great number of students might be present that you will be making an impression on both your students and their parents. You do not want to undo outside of the classroom what you have worked to establish in the classroom.

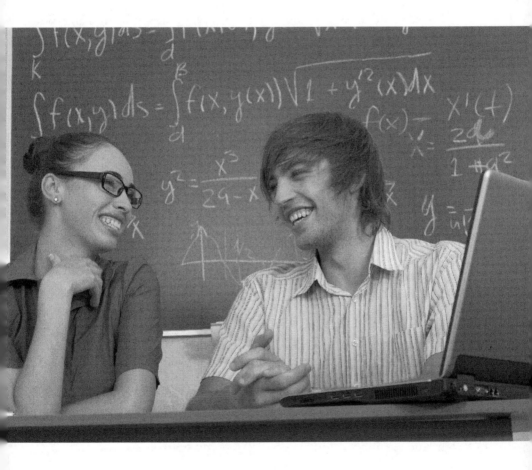

CHAPTER 2
Planning & Preparation

Have you ever heard the saying, "an ounce of preparation is worth a pound of cure"? It is, of course, a common expression that promotes the merits of planning ahead; age-old expressions have so much basic truth to them. This one was quoted by Benjamin Franklin and might be one of the most essential truths any teacher could follow.

As a new teacher, you will report to your "office" (i.e. classroom) well before the first day of school. You will have meetings, planning sessions, and even more meetings on top of that to learn about standard operating procedures, policy changes handed down by your school board, and general goals set by your school's administration. This process is important for you to familiarize yourself with your new school and get comfortable in your new role.

While you attend these meetings, get to know your fellow faculty, and count down the days until your students arrive, your classroom and curriculum planning needs have already begun. No matter what grade you are teaching, you will likely have assigned curriculum and material you need to cover. It is your job to create and execute a lesson plan that allows you to go through that material in a timely manner and ensure all of your students have mastered it by the end of the year. While you will need to remain flexible, the process of lesson planning needs to begin well before the first day of school.

In preparation for your first day of school, you may want to review your student roster and decide if you are going to assign seats or if any of your students have known learning needs (which can range from wearing glasses or having I.E.P plans). You might also want to review your school's code of conduct and decide if there are any rules you want your students to follow beyond those standards. This is an important area to focus your attention on before your students arrive, because you could be playing "catch up" otherwise, losing control of your classroom early on. For specific advice on preparation errors to avoid, read below:

MISTAKE 7

Making the first day all about "fun"...

In your efforts to get to know your students and make them like you, you might be tempted to over-focus on "fun" the first day of school. While it is important to make your students feel welcome, you must immediately communicate the rules and expectations of your classroom and what the consequences will be if these rules are broken.

Since you have determined how you want your students to behave and what consequences of breaking your rules will be, you should communicate these rules/policies to your students right away. I know you want to make a good impression on your students and try to get them into the mindset that learning is fun, but you must remember that your students are coming to school knowing they are supposed to be learning. So, do your best to make them feel comfortable, but do not lull them into thinking the year is going to be easy. Make sure your students know that the school year is going to be challenging but exciting, and you will do all that you can to help them master the material as you learn about some really cool things.

MISTAKE 8
Not defining policies for classroom conduct...

Your students have been in school for several years and likely know how they are expected to behave in a classroom setting. However, if there are rules or procedures you want your students to follow that are specific to your class, you should communicate those immediately.

In order to identify areas to define custom policies, you should think about how you want your students to conduct themselves during tests, how many days will you allow them to complete homework, what the penalty will be if they turn in an assignment late, and so on.

Once you have developed the rules for your classroom, make sure you communicate them both verbally and in writing to your students. Depending on the grade you are teaching, you may or may not want them to take home paperwork for their parents to read and sign in order to ensure their parents understand your rules as well.

MISTAKE 9

Not telling students your academic policies on the first day of school…

At some schools, particularly private institutions, the entire teaching team might have a set way of doing things. At a public school, your department might have standards they expect you to implement. In these instances, follow the rules your team wants you to use and communicate these standards to your class.

If you are allowed to set your own policies/rules regarding things like assignments, late penalties, and individual and group work, make sure you have decided what those rules are going to be, and explain them to your students on the first day of school.

When a student is done with a worksheet, quiz, or test, do you want them to bring it to you and quietly sit in their seat until the class is done? Or do you want them to turn the paper over and wait until you collect the whole classes' tests? What information do you want students to include on each assignment (name, date, class name, period)? Will you allow them to talk while working on individual assignments? Should they ask questions during a lecture or wait for a question and answer period?

No matter what your rules/policies are for your classroom, making sure your students know what to do early in the school year is important. That way, there is no confusion as academic work kicks into full gear.

MISTAKE 10

Not reviewing the student handbook with your students (at least the highlights)...

Do not leave it up to your students to fully understand a student handbook on their own. If you want to adhere strictly to the school's rules and policies, go over the student handbook with your students on the first day of school. Select parts of the student handbook you want them to really understand and spend some extra time on those rules. You can even give your students a little "quiz" on the student handbook to ensure they have read and understood the policies.

MISTAKE 11

Not working a child's needs into your seating arrangements...

Assigning seats for your students will certainly help you learn their names and cultivate a sense of order for your classroom. You can assign seats based on your students' last names (or another organizational system) or allow them to sit where they like and just require them to sit in the same spots each day thereafter.

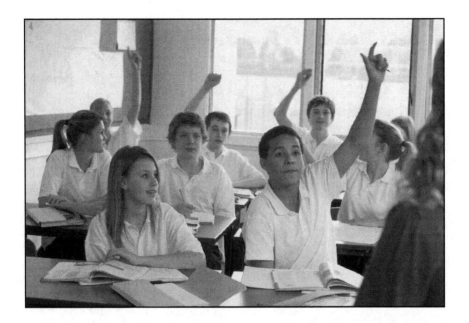

One of the advantages of creating the seating order yourself is that you can setup a neutral arrangement that might be at least somewhat free of clique bias. When doing so, be sure to take into consideration if your students have any needs that would require them to sit toward the front of the room. No matter what seating strategy you employ, make sure you pay attention to how well your students are doing and if any changes are needed.

MISTAKE 12
Not making the most of student orientation...

As part of your preparation for the start of school, you will be expected to participate in a student orientation several days before the first day of class. This will give you an opportunity to meet several students and their parents. Treat this meet-and-greet session as something more than just a chance to shake hands and connect names with faces.

First of all, this gives you an opportunity to hand the paperwork previously discussed directly to the parents. This may or may not increase the likelihood that it will be read and digested by the parents, but any chance you get to communicate with your student's parents is one you should take. Creating open dialogue early in the process should make things easier if you and the parents ever need to address a serious academic or behavioral issue.

The next thing you can do is to ask parents to fill out a little "tell me about your child" questionnaire. Some parents might not want to do this, but many parents (well, moms at least) would love to tell you about their teens and provide you with additional insight about their child prior to the start of the school year. Allowing them this opportunity will give you a chance to get to know more about your future students and perhaps even help you plan better for the first day of class.

Finally, this is an opportunity to connect with your parents and discuss things like school supplies and what the students need to bring from home on a daily basis. Even though they know that many teachers spend their own money on classroom supplies, parents can resent the amount of money they need to spend on school supplies at the start of each school year. Discussing what your students will need the most and what they will be using the supplies for can help bring the parents around. Just remember not to ask for anything truly extravagant if you can make do with something simpler. Parents probably would not like the idea of you spending your hard-earned money on crayons and paper, but they are equally unlikely to want to buy modeling clay for "artsy" type projects.

MISTAKE 13

Not anticipating extra students in your class the first day of school...

Last-minute registrations are a given. In high school, students might even change their schedules around at the last minute to accommodate a different class or help them meet a graduation requirement. For whatever reason, your class roster may not be the same when school begins as when you first showed up to work. As a result, you should be prepared to add or lose students that first week of school.

This means you should make a few extras of whatever handouts or work you are going to disperse. Be prepared to rearrange your seating setup if your added students need to sit toward the front of the class. Basically, be comfortable with the fact that your best laid-out plans might be at least partially swept aside for late additions or changes to your student body.

MISTAKE 14

Not knowing if one of your students have special needs...

Not all "special needs" children are assigned to special education teachers. There is a chance that you will have a student with ADHD, dyslexia, or difficulty seeing/hearing. If your students have learning or testing needs that you need to take into consideration — make sure you do so. Failing to comply with their special learning needs could make you subject to a lawsuit. If you can, identify students with special needs early in the year, and adjust your policies/teaching strategies accordingly.

MISTAKE 15

Not evaluating your students' strengths and weaknesses…

As I previously mentioned, you will have students join your class at the last minute or even later. These students may have joined you from a different school system, a private school (or public school if you are a private school teacher), or a home school environment. In fact, even the students you know you will have in your classroom on the first day of school might not have attended your school the prior school year.

Students from a wide range of school setups might mean that your students had different learning experiences and will start the school year with different knowledge and skill sets. Outside of curriculum, there are other influences that could impact what your students know and what they need to learn, ranging from contributions by the parents to summer camp activities.

For these reasons, it is important for you to quickly assess and understand what skills, knowledge, and tools your students already possess and what they still need to master. The earlier you identify areas where your students might need extra help, the faster you can bring them up to speed and advance the whole class together.

I recommend that you evaluate your students' abilities and knowledge the first week of school, and adjust your curriculum however necessary to accommodate what you deem from these assessments. This should make your whole school year run more smoothly.

MISTAKE 16

Not reviewing previous year's material…

Since you are teaching middle or high school students, you can be sure your children are not new to the classroom or learning experience. They all come into your class with a perceived level of understanding they should have achieved the previous year. However, as all parents have experienced, the ability of a child to remember what we want them to forget and to forget what we want them to remember knows no bounds.

For this reason, either before or after you perform a skills assessment, you should plan several review sessions for your students. You can either conduct a review session first to wake their little minds up from the summer slump and then evaluate their skill sets when you think they are firing on more cylinders. Or conversely, you can assess what they retained and prepare your review sessions on what you learn. Either way, a review of subject matter basics at the very least should prove valuable to advancing your student's mastery and performance for the year to come.

MISTAKE 17

Not keeping things simple…

Have you heard the acronym K.I.S.S.? It stands for keep it simple, stupid. The idea is that most systems work best if they are kept simple. This principle translates well for teaching. Whether you are instructing your students on the first day of school or leading them through a series of tests, be sure to keeps things simple and straightforward for them.

CHAPTER 3
Fairness & Consistency

Whew! You made it through your first day/week of school — it should be all downhill from here. OK, not really. Putting student faces with the names on your roster was the easy part — now the work begins. The first thing you must realize is that whether you are teaching children through those "in-between" years of middle school or teens on the cusp of adulthood in high school, you will both be dealing with personalities that are highly formed and will influence these students their entire lives.

You must accept that they are largely who they are going to be without forgetting that you can still have a strong impact on their learning experience and desire to learn. Your best and worst moments may very well be remembered for decades to come, even when your students are grown and working in a wide-range of professional fields.

Understanding that you are important to these students without presuming that you can really alter their natural personalities is vital step in ensuring your success as a teacher. At some point in time, you probably took a Myers-Briggs personality test and can tell if you are an ESTJ or an INFP or one of the other 14 personality types this test qualifies.

However, you might be surprised to learn that there are dozens of personality tests that can be administered for children. From tests that will code a child as a lion, beaver, otter, or golden retriever to those that will tell you if a child is choleric, sanguine, melancholy, or phlegmatic. I am not advocating one particular coding system over another or suggesting that you give your students personality tests. I am simply reminding you that much of a child's personality is determined from birth.

Therefore, the student in your classroom that is extremely talkative is probably not trying to drive you crazy, but is that way because that is how they process information. Another teen who gets upset when stories do not have a happy ending or when you discuss tragedies such as the attacks on 9/11 might not be emotionally unstable, but just a highly sensitive child.

Throughout your teaching career, you will encounter personalities in children/teens that gel well with your own and are easy for you to teach and ones that grate on your nerves in a way you never would have thought possible. You must learn to manage and work with diverse personalities as a teacher because you will likely encounter them all.

Try to remember that diversity is the spice of life and managing all of these personalities is one of the key leadership skills that will mark your success as a teacher. In fact, at several points in this book, I will emphasize and discuss the differences between students that can span personality, race, culture, gender, puberty, and so much more. However, though all of your students are unique, you need to ensure there is no perception that you are favoring or discriminating against any subset of students. This chapter emphasizes how fair and consistent treatment will benefit you in classroom management.

Student Equality

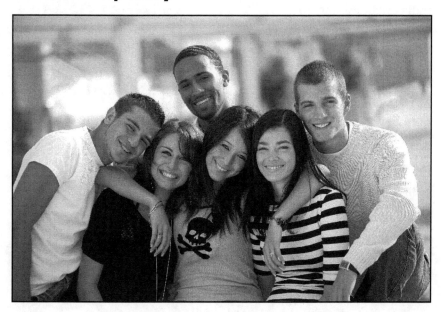

In a later portion of this book, I will dedicate a considerable amount of space to the relationships you form with your students and if you want to be perceived as a hard/strict teacher or a pushover. However, I cannot in good faith discuss discipline in the classroom without going over some basic classroom management strategies for maintaining control.

You probably already realize you will have problem students, which can range from a disrespectful child to the "class clown." Dealing with students who disrupt your lessons may be more difficult than teaching the material itself. You must manage outbursts with professionalism while taking steps to minimize how often these interruptions occur.

What you might not realize is that it is not just the "bad" students who can sidetrack your lesson — very good, curious students can do it as well. While I was too quiet and shy in school to be this child, I am most certainly the mother of two such students. Either of my children could charm the pants off a teacher while taking over their class — without really even meaning to.

When a child is naturally curious about a concept or lesson you are teaching, it is easy to get caught up in that teaching moment. After all, this is your dream! A student is engaged and really interested in what you are teaching, the student is asking challenging questions, and he or she seems genuinely interested in the answers. Frankly, you need to be able to leave your lesson plan behind for a moment or two when the class shows an interest in something and gives you an opportunity to go into greater depth.

However, as tempting as it would be to go off on a learning tangent every time the opportunity arises, you have to keep your lesson plans more or less on track. And if you deviate from those plans, it needs to be at your discretion when you feel it would benefit the majority of your students. The following are recommendations on how to keep control of your classroom when children become disruptive for any reason:

MISTAKE 18
Letting "gifted" children direct the class…

Gifted or advanced students can run the gamut in their personalities; some will be shy and quiet while others will be very outgoing and talkative. Every now and then, you will run into one who is charming and curious and will be able to all too easily dictate how the class goes if you let them.

Assuming they are not "know-it-alls" who think they know more than you do, you will probably enjoy these students in your classroom. You will enjoy the questions they ask and knowing that if you call on them, they will likely have the answer or at least something interesting to say. These students will likely make straight A's — or close to it — and will make you look good on tests and evaluations that could impact your job.

However, it is for the benefit of the entire class that you not allow these students to become "teacher's pets." You do not want to appear to favor these students over others, because that will hurt your ability to engage your entire class. Furthermore, while many advanced children/teens find it easy to interact with adults, they still need to be able to function well among their peers. Being perceived as a "favorite" with the teacher may not benefit them with the other students.

On the other hand, you do not want to stifle these students or their desire to learn. Therefore, find ways to manage their participation in your classroom. Rather than ask if anyone knows the answer to a question, group the children together on "teams" and divide up the students that are more likely to know the answers so that each team will be able to take turns answering questions correctly.

If you are lecturing or doing a presentation, tell the students to take notes and write questions on a note card or piece of paper. Then at the end of your presentation, collect the papers in a box and pull out five to discuss as a class. You can bypass any card or paper left blank and just address the questions you find. Once you complete this discussion period, tell the students that can ask you additional questions after school.

Employing these strategies allows you to control the pace and direction of your class while still engaging your more advanced students. Additionally, it protects them from gaining a "know-it-all" reputation among their peers that is not always desirable.

MISTAKE 19

Letting "big" personalities overshadow you…

In the previous scenario, the "gifted" student might have a big personality, but they are not the only child who can overshadow you in the classroom. From the overly disruptive student to the "class clown," there are several "big" personalities that can seize control of your classroom if you let them. You need to identify early on who these students are, and make sure you have strategies in mind on how to manage these children so you do not find yourself trying to wrestle control back from them later in the school year.

Children and teens seek attention in many ways for a wide variety of reasons, and all too often, adults overlook bad behavior believing that the children in question just need a little attention and everything will be fine. It would be nice to think that any teen that is "acting up" in your classroom just needs a little positive attention and reinforcement, and if you give it to them, all will be well. However, that is not always the case.

It might not be your attention the student is seeking at all. It could be the attention of their parents, the focus of a girl or boy that they like, or just popularity among their peers. Some teens might believe that if they can make the class laugh, everyone will like them. Or they could be using "clowning around" as a cover for hiding a learning deficiency, inability to read, or other things that make them feel inadequate.

You want to make sure that you pay attention to the reasons why the individual child is behaving in the manner they are, and ensure that you use the proper discipline measures to not lose control of your classroom. A disruptive student might need to sit by him or herself for a while or be sent to the principal's office if they cannot be quiet. A student who is clowning around might need to be separated from his or her audience. If the class is not functioning well in the midst of one activity, you might need to change activities to calm your students down.

MISTAKE 20
Making a student feel "small" in order to put them in their place…

Do not be tempted to try to "put a child in their place" with inappropriate comments or sarcasm. Even if the student is acting a little too grown up and doing their best to act like they are the one in charge, you need to settle them down without hurting their feelings or making them feel bad. In fact, perhaps the best way to demonstrate to all the students in your class that you are in control is to remain calm and professional while you work to restore order.

One thing to understand about personalities is that some people are predisposed to avoid conflict or to be non-confrontational. If you know that you are one of these types of people, be prepared to be a little harder and firmer with your students than you would normally feel comfortable being.

Some teens will push limits and test boundaries just to see what happens. These children can be well managed if you establish rules, be firm in consequences, and be consistent with punishments. If you relent on a few occasions, these types of students might push back to see if you will give in again. Just make sure you always back up what you say, because these children will notice when you fail to do so.

MISTAKE 21

Being too hard on kids who talk too much...

While it is important to maintain control of your classroom, you should be careful on how you deal with students who are too talkative, particularly those who want to talk about academic subjects. If a teen is whispering to a friend about their favorite television show or a boy/girl that they like, that is the kind of talking you should absolutely silence.

However, if a student is talking about school subjects and asking questions, you need to carefully instruct them to be quiet and tell them you will go over some of their questions later. Many teens are far too shy to answer a teacher's questions in class. Others are quick to raise their hands and always want to show how smart they are. You need to make sure you can engage the reluctant participants without stifling the natural participatory instincts of those who are willing to speak out.

Imagine that you have a naturally curious student who enjoys answering or asking questions and feels no awkwardness when it comes time for class discussion. However, if you are critical of this student — particularly in front of the class — you will gradually create a scenario where he does so less and less as the year goes on. By the end of the year, you notice he is not raising his hand anymore and has gone from being gregarious to quiet.

The lesson has stuck. The once vibrant, excited learner has become a student who is quiet and not likely to volunteer in class. He will meekly give answers when called upon by future teachers, and he will continue to get good grades, but some of his enthusiasm for learning has been squelched. Would you want to be teacher that caused this?

You have the opportunity to teach teens about situational timing, that there is a time and place for certain kinds of behavior, and that sometimes you have to be patient and wait until the right moment to talk and ask questions.

If you have a student that is distracting you from progressing through a lesson by asking a lot of questions, try designating a question and answer or discussion period at the end of the lesson. Have your students write down their questions as they think of them, and then they can ask any that you might not have covered once the lecture is finished. This will allow the "talkative" student a chance to ask their questions in an appropriate format while also learning about adhering to the structure of a classroom.

MISTAKE 22
Mixing it up with the class clown…

If you are a bit of a jokester yourself, when a student starts cracking jokes or clowning around, you might be tempted to joke around with them. It is certainly fine to tell some jokes and make your students laugh from time to time. However, you also need to maintain an aura of professionalism that lets the students know you are *not* "one of them."

I know as a teacher you want to be liked, and you might even be one of those adults that find "burping" and "farting" noises funny. On some occasions, your "clown" might even crack some very funny jokes. You may smile, but you should be cautious not to get caught up in the laughter of the classroom. It will be hard enough to regain control of a bunch of raucous teens once the giggles take hold — it will not be easier if you are having a good belly laugh as well.

Also, if one of your students cracks a joke that might be considered "at your expense," you should be sure not to joke back using them as the "punch line." You should be made of thicker skin than your students can hope to muster. Do not take any of their jokes or comments personally, and make sure you maintain the aura of a manager at all times.

Finally, be cautious of unintended connotations connected to some jokes. Ensure that any joke you do make does not have any negative gender, racial, or religious stereotypes included. Teens can be highly sensitive, so it is best to err on the side of caution and not risk offending anyone. Remember, even if your students are not offended or miss the biased part of the joke, if they repeat it to their parents — and they will — their parents might get upset and contact your principal. It is just best to avoid this scenario altogether.

MISTAKE 23
Responding harshly to a disrespectful student...

Every generation has their "walked two miles to school, in the snow, uphill, both ways" stories. I believe another version of that is "if I said/did that, my parents would have...." Nevertheless, it is a common perception today that teens are more disrespectful, know swear words earlier than they once did, and may be more likely to use them.

If that perception is correct, the probability that you might have a student or two talk back to you or perhaps even curse at you seems far higher than when you were a student. When a teen speaks to you as if they were an adult, it might be very tempting to speak back to them as if they were an adult. You should resist that urge.

When a student is disrespectful, you should remain calm, professional, and above all else, in control. Whatever your policy is to deal with disruptive students, put those procedures into practice. Isolate the child quickly so his/her negative behavior does not spread to other students. If you need to send a child to the principal's office, do so before the interruption gets out of hand.

Just be careful not to yell, curse, or insult the child in your efforts to establish yourself as the dominant personality in the room. You want to maintain control of the classroom and of your emotions. Doing so will ensure that the non-disruptive students respect you while showing the disrespectful student that he or she is not going to get under your skin or provoke you.

MISTAKE 24

Overcompensating for your perceived shortcomings…

You have heard of the Napoleon complex, a type of psychological phenomenon that is said to exist in short people where they seek to overcompensate for insecurities caused by their short nature. I have heard of short female teachers who operated like little dictators because even by middle school, their students already started towering over them.

These teachers somehow developed terrifying reputations with their students. They were not liked or loved, but they were feared, which seems to be the goal. At a glance, it appears these teachers are taking the philosophy of "speak softly, but carry a big stick" a little too far.

If there is some area that you perceive as being a weak point for you, address it as best you can, but do not let it dominate your concerns. You should work to highlight your strengths rather than worrying about covering up your weaknesses. With a good amount of planning and preparation, you can shrink your weaknesses to a point where your students will not notice them.

Understand that your students walk into the classroom assuming you are in charge. While some of them might try to push the boundaries and see if you mean what you say, they still walk in expecting you to be the one they need to try to challenge — that automatically means they respect you as the "boss" of the class. Your goal will be to not lose that respect.

As a new teacher, you might be younger than many of the other teachers and parents you work with. Do not let that be something that makes you insecure. If you maintain your professionalism and do your job well, before long, no one will notice your age.

While your children will probably not be perceptive enough to realize if you are exercising a Napoleon complex or some version thereof, coworkers, supervisors, and parents will notice. If you are too extreme, the very thing you think is keeping the respect of your students might cost you that of your parents and colleagues.

MISTAKE 25

Letting bathroom breaks get out of hand...

Compared to the other subjects I covered in this chapter, managing bathroom breaks probably seems out of place. However, students love to push limits, and if you are not careful, something as mundane as a bathroom break can completely derail your lesson plan for the day.

While you certainly do not want a student to have an accident in your classroom, a series of bathroom breaks should probably be viewed with a suspicious eye. You should try to make note of patterns that your students demonstrate. If the same students always ask to go the bathroom in close proximity to each other, you may be correct to assume the bathroom break is not related to their bladder needs.

Remember that it is reasonable for you to assume that students have the time to make bathroom stops in between classes and that your class should not always become the "bathroom break" period. On the other hand, be mindful that occasionally girls will need to go to the bathroom more frequently than normal, and you will need to be accommodating to help them avoid an embarrassing accident.

Just be sure to balance the desire not to have a student have an accident in your classroom with the need not to be taken advantage of by your class. If you suspect bathroom privileges are being abused, talk with the student privately. Let them know you will expect them to go to the bathroom before your class begins, and you will count them as tardy if they cannot do so and make it to your class on time.

Avoiding Inconsistencies

One of the most common pieces of advice parenting magazines offer is that children need consistency. As cliché as this guiding principal may seem, being consistent in your classroom will serve you well. Your teens are well aware of the things that make them different and having an odd color hair, wearing glasses, having braces, or even being left-handed can make them feel like they stand out in a negative way.

If you allow yourself to be inconsistent with how you treat your students, you could alienate some of them without even realizing it. You know that while all students are equal, they are not the same — some of them will be brighter than others, some of them will be more athletically gifted, others will be prettier, and some will just possess an air of likability. If you are being honest with yourself, you will like some of your students better than others. However, you can never let that show. You must make your students believe that only you care about one thing — educating all of them to the best of your ability.

Along with avoiding inconsistencies in how you treat one student from another, you should avoid irregularity in how you manage your classroom. Certainly, there are many things in your personal life that can impact your work. It is acceptable to have some minor deviations in your day-to-day teaching efforts based on whether or not you are having a bad day or woke up feeling monumentally inspired with just the right idea on how to communicate a concept to your students. It is, however, a poor teacher who behaves erratically from week to week, enforcing rules one time while letting things slide another.

If you want your students to respect you, then follow your rules and demonstrate their best behavior; you need to condition them on what to expect. If you are unpredictable and they are left guessing as to what the consequence of an action will be, they might be unable to decide if the action is one they wish to take or bypass. Being consistent in how you handle the same situation with every student and situation will help your students understand that you mean what you say and that you are to be respected. The following mistakes are ones you should avoid, even if you do not currently understand why. Consider the advice below:

MISTAKE 26
Being relaxed one day and firm the next.

The way you manage your classroom during the year is the way your students will expect you to manage it all year long. If you begin in a relaxed manner, it will be difficult to become stricter later in the year if you do not have as much control over your classroom as you might like. If you joke and laugh with the students about poor behavior one day, the children in your class will expect you to always overlook such conduct. Letting small violations pass will only confuse students later if you try to enforce harder standards.

Furthermore, if you are strict for several days, lighten up, then become strict again, you will utterly confound the students in your classroom. You will leave them lacking understanding in how to behave and what to expect from you. While your change in teaching style and/or mood could be completely independent of the students and simply a product of your personal life, you will still leave the students wondering if they are somehow causing the changes you are demonstrating.

In the worst possible scenario, your shifting mood and teaching style could damage your ability to teach effectively. If you want to protect your ability to positively impact your students and communicate your lesson plan, you will want to minimize anything that could distract from the education process. Among many other things that could have a negative impact, your inconsistent behavior is at the top of the list. When students are left wondering how the teacher will act from one week to the next, they are not fully focused on learning. You will want to limit how often this occurs.

MISTAKE 27

Showing favoritism…

As I have previously mentioned, you can go ahead and draw the conclusion that you will have favorite students. While a parent might be able to hold off from favoring one child over another if they have only a few children, in a classroom with 25 students or more, it is very likely you will have ones you like better than others. You might even have a student or two that you look at and think, *"My job would be so much easier if they were all like him (her)."*

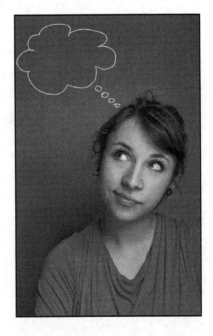

There is nothing wrong with feeling that way inside. The mistake you must avoid is showing your feelings of favoritism to the student and/or the class. There are many reasons you should avoid favoritism, besides the clear lack of professionalism it denotes. You might want to consider that favor from you could turn into claims of racism or sexism if a parent decides to bring it to your principal's attention that you are not being fair in your teaching practice. The first reason to avoid favoritism is that it could be used against you in a complaint.

The possibility that such a complaint could get out of hand — *Ms. Smith does not like black students; Mr. Jones does not treat the girls the same as the boys* — only worsens the professional hit you might take. Please remember that while most people realize that children and parents are capable of complaining for no reason—you are a new teacher. Your principal, administrators, and school board do not know you as well as a seasoned veteran. It is best to be cautious early in your career and avoid mistakes that could lead people to forming negative opinions of you.

Showing favoritism could also limit your teaching impact on your entire classroom. First, you could create over-confidence in the students whom you favor, enabling them to believe that they are "better than" or "more deserving" than their counterparts. Second, demonstrating favor to your students could lead some of them to conclude that you do not care if they master the material just as long as your "favorites" do. Always calling on one or two students because you know they know the answer could lead some students to stop trying to answer questions or feeling too embarrassed to volunteer. You must strike a balance between rewarding those students who perform well and propping up the children/teens in your classroom that need extra assistance.

MISTAKE 28

Showing dislike for a student...

On the flip side of the same coin of favoritism is showing disdain for any one student or group of students. The first thing you should probably ask yourself is if you do have any preconceived ideas about people based on race, gender, and religion. You should ask yourself if you are prepared to teach children of all races, religions, and even sexual orientations.

Depending on the size of the town or the area of the country you live in, the diversity issues you will encounter in your classroom could range significantly. But the chance that you will teach minorities of any and all kinds certainly exists. Whether the child in your classroom is raised as an atheist or is transgender, you will need to maintain a level of professionalism in your classroom (protecting these children from bullying and harassment), while not communicating any negative private thoughts you might have to the student.

A likely possibility is that you will simply have teens in your classroom that you dislike. Perhaps one of your students is a bit of a "mean girl," and she brings back memories of your own mistreatment in middle or high school. You could have a "jock" in your class that acts more like a bully, and while you are able to control his behavior through threat of punishment, you are unable to get him to interact with other teens in a positive manner. You could have a child/teen who never turns in homework, does poorly on tests, and just does not seem to care about anything you are trying to teach.

Regardless of how much you dislike a student, do not show it — not to the student or class. The first thing you should keep in mind is that even if you do not reach that student in the first month or several months of school, you could still make an impact by the end of the year. Do not rob yourself of the victory of teaching a child that others would give up on. You must also hold the most difficult, problematic child in your classroom as an example to all the others. If you care about that child, then you care about them all. This is a message that your students will pick up on and internalize whether you realize it or not.

Of course, my warning not to show dislike to a student does not suggest that you should not discipline a problem student. However, this is about avoiding inconsistencies. When a problem student breaks the rule, handle him or her in the same way you would if any other student did so. Do not be harder on some students and easier on others. If you operate your classroom in a consistent manner, students will be less likely to pick up on who is your favorite student and worst nightmare. Approach the parents in much the same way, and you will build yourself a reputation for being fair and just, as well as a good teacher.

MISTAKE 29

Using sarcasm...

All right, if sarcasm is a second language for you, you are not going to like this section much. Heck, it is not my favorite talking point either. In fact, when I first read Katie Hurley's "Want to Stop Mean Girls? Raise Nice Girls, Instead," article, and I got to that particular piece of advice, I rolled my eyes.

Then I thought more about what she was saying, and I read the article again. Hurley is a Child and Adolescent Psychotherapist and wrote this article about her efforts to start a "friendship club" among fourth grade girls at the school she was working. This was brought on as a response to teachers asking her for help with girl students whose relationship troubles with each other were interrupting the classroom.

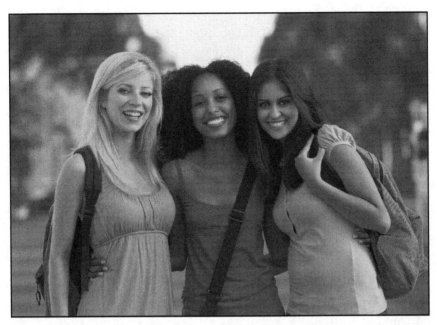

The program was successful, and one key element she sites is cutting down on "cutting comments" between the girls. If this is effective between elementary-aged children, it will be effective in your effort to relate to the students.

First off, students will not always understand your sarcastic comments or that you were attempting to be comedic instead of insulting. This misunderstanding will undoubtedly lead to difficulties as you work to impart your lessons on the class. Whether the student is just hurt and does not listen to the rest of your lesson or the student thinks you meant something else entirely, you will have failed in your communications with one or more of the children in your care.

Instead, say what you mean in a clear and concise way. Be patient with a student who is sarcastic or "smart" with you, and do not respond in kind.

CHAPTER 4
Discipline Strategies

Let us assume that you have already decided what the rules of your classroom are going to be and have defined a behavioral system to explain to your students the first day of school. Now you must address the ever-difficult task of deciding how to discipline your students when the situation warrants.

In all likelihood, your school has some discipline standards established, such as detention for skipping class or sending students home for wearing inappropriate clothing. More serious offenses like fighting or bullying might earn suspensions. Those disciplinary steps will be easy for you to follow.

However, there are smaller offenses that you have to decide how to handle. When a student talks out of turn or causes a disruption in your classroom by clowning around, you must decide if such behavior will earn the student a trip to the principal's office or after-school detention. You must decide if you will have a warning system and what it will be. As you figure these things out, do not hesitate to consult your fellow teachers to see what they do in their classrooms. If you watch enough examples and receive good advice, then you will be able to sort out what works best for you.

In the meantime, as you seek to develop your discipline policy, there are some things you should remember NOT to do; these errors range from disciplinary action you should never use to things that will just give you a headache if you do not avoid them. This chapter is dedicated to covering how to maintain control of your classroom while avoiding a wide-range of disciplinary mistakes.

Ways Not to Discipline — Ever

There are many mistakes you can make your first year of teaching (and even beyond) that may affect you professionally. However, there are a few that will likely get you fired or at least reprimanded by your superiors. It should be your highest priority to avoid committing these mistakes. Read below for the mistakes that are related to discipline:

MISTAKE 30

Using ridicule to get a student in line…

If you have a sarcastic personality or caustic sense of humor, it would be easy to make snide comments when one of your students gets out of line or responds poorly to a question asked in class. As natural as that is to you, I highly recommend that you avoid engaging students in this manner.

There are several reasons why you should avoid ridiculing a child in class. The first is that it is more likely to cause you to lose control of your classroom than to keep it. Students will laugh at almost any joke you crack — at least all of the ones they understand. When laughter breaks out in your classroom, calming the students down will take some effort. If the students are laughing at another child, the lack of classroom control can rise as the student you made the snide comment to reacts in anger or tears — both of which are possible if you engage in the behavior. Whatever you hoped to achieve with your comment, if you thought about it at all, will probably not be accomplished, and there will be negative results.

The second thing that will happen after a snide comment is that you will seriously damage your professional image with the students and parents who hear about the incident. The last thing you need to do is allow one small comment to injure your reputation as a professional. If you were working at an office among other adults, you might be able to make a snide comment without consequence if you do not let it happen very often, but students will not understand and neither will their parents. Once you have lowered their opinion and respect for you, it will be difficult to regain confidence and control of your classroom. Teaching and relationship building will become more challenging, and some parents will be looking for other signs that you are not doing your job well. Basically, you will stack the deck of cards against yourself and make you job harder than it needs to be.

If you are tempted to ridicule a student to stop them from making fun of or teasing another child in your classroom, you should think twice about adopting such tactics. While this might seem like a good way to defend the child who is being teased and could serve to make the "bully" understand what it is like to be laughed at, it is far more likely that you will only create an atmosphere where you drag yourself down to the level of the children you teach. The older your students are, the more damaging this could be to your ability to lead your classroom effectively. Once your students start to think of you as being "one of them" or "on their level," you have basically lost your ability to be their leader. In instances such as this, it is far more important for you to set an example of how to handle a "bully" with self-control than to try to put the child in his or her place using ridicule.

In addition to the damage you can do to your relationship with your students as a whole, you will permanently fail the student you ridiculed. Whatever reason you have for wanting to bring the child back in line with a snide comment, you must not overlook the fact that it is your responsibility to teach all of the students in your classroom. Disciplining a student who disrupts your teaching allows you to send a message that your instruction is important, and you are not to be interrupted. Ridiculing a child sends another message altogether. It conveys the idea that the lesson is not important, and you are willing to abandon your teaching to talk condescendingly to one of your students. While that student might not act out again, he or she will not likely seek your help if he or she needs it for fear of more ridicule. Furthermore, other students might be equally unlikely to ask for help, because they do not want you to make fun of them. This means you have not just damaged your ability to control your classroom; you have decreased your ability to effectively do your job.

Finally, it is not wise to use ridicule or snide comments to try to get a student to perform better academically. If a student answers your question with a smart remark or even an incredibly stupid comment that shows they were not paying attention to what you were saying, your job is to keep your composure and not make the child feel dumb. As in the above scenario, making a child feel stupid will not just decrease the likelihood that one student will feel comfortable participating in class, but it will lower the chances that any of your students will want to respond to your questions.

Furthermore, you must not respond to a question from a student in a snide or negative manner. You may think that the saying "there are no stupid questions" is completely false. There are, in fact, many stupid questions, and you will probably hear dozens of them throughout your first year of teaching. No matter how much a student's question makes you wonder if he or she is even listening to you talk, you cannot answer them in a sarcastic or mean way. You have to remain professional and address their questions completely, no matter how tedious this task can be. If you do not adopt this philosophy, your students might stop asking questions — even when they do not understand the material. If they stop asking questions, you might find yourself wondering why they are performing badly on homework and tests. Maintaining an environment that encourages questions and learning will be the key to your success. Do not sabotage yourself with a sarcastic or snide comment — no matter how funny it sounds in your head.

MISTAKE 31

Cursing...

Almost every parent understands how easy it is to lose your temper with his or her children, especially when it comes to yelling or cursing at them. Of course, just about every parent who has done this realizes that losing composure with a child does not gain you respect or make the child more likely to obey you. Simply put, while yelling and/or cursing might seem like a good way to let off steam and let your students know you "mean business," this will demonstrate poor professionalism.

Whether cursing is acceptable in an office setting varies on the office, the company, the manager, and the curse words that are used. A four-letter word at one company might not get you in trouble, but could land you in sensitivity training at another corporation. Cursing at work could negatively impact the impression you make on your boss and coworkers. When I advised clients in career management, I tell them to completely avoid it in an interview and limit it as much as possible in a new position.

In a school environment, you need to completely remove curse words from your vocabulary — even if your students know more profanities than you do. While your class has probably heard everything you could think to say, it is still the essence of a professional teacher to avoid the use of vulgar language at school.

If a parent hears you curse or brings it to your principal's attention that you are cursing and yelling at your students, you will almost certainly earn yourself an official reprimand. If you say a curse word that could have sexual or sexist implications, you might receive a significantly more serious punishment. As long as you are the new kid on the block, avoid using language that will make your principal wonder if he or she made the right choice in hiring you.

MISTAKE 32

Yelling...

You might be thinking, *"Ok, I can raise my voice without cursing. Then the students will know I mean business without me getting myself in trouble."*

You could use this approach, but I think you will find children do not respond well when adults lose their composure. Young children want to know the adult in charge of them is in control of the situation; screaming and yelling does not convey control of your classroom. Older children will lose respect for you once they learn they can get you riled up and off track from teaching. Some of them might even try to make you upset on purpose just because they know it is possible.

Keeping your composure in the classroom is about more than just maintaining professionalism or not giving parents a reason to question your qualifications to do your job. Remaining calm and restoring order in your classroom, even when things start to get out of hand, is about making sure the students know you are always in the lead. When you calmly handle a mounting situation without letting it rile you, students can see that you are in control of the classroom, and they will respond accordingly.

One of the most important ways you can keep control of your classroom, without getting to the point of losing your cool and yelling at your students, is to not let little things mount up. When you ignore small issues of misbehavior or let "little things" slide, some students will continue to test you to see how far they can push you before you respond and do something. If you address misdeeds early on with increasing forms of discipline as the offense increases, you can let your students know you mean business without reaching a level of frustration that will lead to yelling and screaming. So be sure to address issues early, and do not let them build up. This should help you remain calm and professional even as students test the limits of your patience.

MISTAKE 33
Getting physical…

School spankings are more or less a thing of the past. Even in Catholic schools, you no longer hear about nuns hitting children with rulers or any other form of physical punishment. If you are of the "spare the rod, spoil the child" thinking, understand that there are many, many reasons that schools have backed off corporal punishment, and it is best for your career that you follow suit.

First, for students old enough to have been subject to physical punishment in school, it often ranks among their worst experiences with teachers. Stephen Klubock, a Career Coach and Account Manager (who happens to also be a military veteran), described his two worst teachers as his third grade teacher who would hit her ruler across their knuckles and his second grade teacher who would shake them in the supply closet to get them in line.

Decades later, he remembers those teachers not for what they instructed, but for how they behaved. The obvious lesson to be imparted here is that you do not want the only reason some child remembers you to be because you back-handed them for ill behavior.

The argument against getting physical with a student is about more than just making a bad impression on your students for years to come. There is also the fact that what parents consider acceptable in terms of physical punishment varies widely, and you do not want to do something to a child that a parent might consider abusive. You can rest assured that 99 percent of the time, it is going to be best to keep your hands off the child when it comes to discipline.

On the very rare occasion where you might be called on to restrain one student from hurting another, you should still avoid physically striking a student. Not only could this behavior hurt you professionally, but it could get you sued. Slapping, pushing, or hitting a student is just not worth it, no matter how bad you might think they deserve it. If it comes to this, remove the child from your classroom immediately, and give yourself and the rest of your students a chance to calm down.

Small-Time Discipline Measures

You understand the importance of maintaining control of your classroom, and you are well aware of the fact that you will encounter behavior for which your students need to be punished. The previous section details some big mistakes you should not make. And of course, you can rest assured that you can send children to the principal's office for major offenses such as fighting, bullying, and suspicion of substance abuse. However, you still might be confused, unsure, or even worried about how to handle minor disciplinary issues.

You have several options available to you on the disciplinary front when it comes to minor disruptions and student mistakes. There are times when a stern look, a firmer tone of voice (commonly referred to as your "teacher's voice"), or any number of other symbolic gestures that you have trained your students to recognize as a signal to be quiet.

In the moments when your students are more wound up, (such as days when they know there is going to be a class party or any day during the month of December) you might have to alter your lesson plan and engage your students in an activity that will capture their attention and tie into the subject you are trying to impart.

When you must use disciplinary tactics for one or two students, do so in a way that disrupts your class as little as possible, and be sure to focus your correction on the child's behavior, not them. I say this to help you build a positive relationship with that child overall, but also to ensure that you will be able to work with the child's parents if the need arises. Read on to familiarize yourself with some mistakes to avoid when disciplining students for minor classroom offenses.

MISTAKE 34

Sending students to the office over small matters…

As a new teacher, you might be unsure about when to send children to the principal's office, and you might even be tempted to use the experience to get "problem" students to straighten up. You also might think that if you have gone through your color-coded behavioral system, sending a child to the principal's office is the appropriate next step, regardless of the seriousness of the offense.

You should keep in mind that a referral to the office should be a serious disciplinary step, and you will bolster your creditability as a classroom manager if you do not use it over small offenses. Consider putting the following things on a "do not send" list for your students:

- Not doing homework
- Marking on desks
- Making rude comments or talking excessively
- Being occasionally tardy
- Not doing classwork or failing to pay attention
- Chewing gum or eating in class
- Sleeping in class

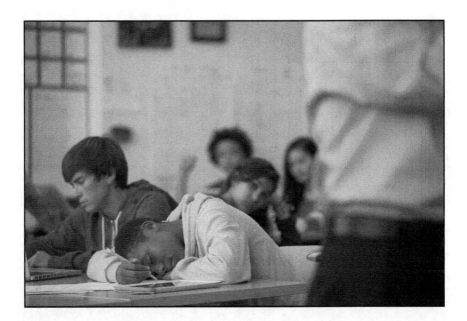

For many of these issues, you can handle them in class or after school. You can quietly wake a child up or ask them to throw their gum away. You can address a student being tardy with the child and then the parents if you are concerned their tardiness will have a negative impact on their studies.

A stern look, being separated from other students, and/or detention might be enough to get disruptive or talkative children to behave. In regards to those not doing their homework or class work, you can dock their grades accordingly. If you are concerned about them failing, contact their parents and schedule a meeting. As long as the student is not disrupting the class, the lack of effort might not be something you can change, but it does not necessarily mean a trip to see the principal either.

MISTAKE 35
Not knowing your school's unexcused tardy/absence policy…

I may have just cautioned you not to send students to see the administrator for being occasionally tardy, but I also have to remind you that your school/school district most likely has a policy on how many unexcused tardy and absent days they will tolerate before there are negative consequences for the student.

In some areas, if a student misses too many school days, they cannot advance to the next grade level regardless of the quality of their work. There are schools where too many tardy markings will count as an unexcused absence against the student. You should monitor these markings and let the students and their parents know if they are in any danger of the attendance — or lack thereof — causing them to fail a grade.

You should also know when your school will expect you to refer a student to the principal for habitual tardiness. Just be sure to follow your school's policy so that if something comes up later, you cannot be considered culpable in the student's ignorance in the matter.

MISTAKE 36

Using classroom control measures that could cause more disruption...

Despite the fact that your lesson might have contained zero humor or jokes in it, teens can pretty much find a reason to laugh at just about anything if the mood strikes them. And these fits of laughter are more contagious than the common cold. When you want to use a single or method to get your students to be silent and settle down, be sure not to use one that could cause the children/teens to become more rowdy.

One example might be if you are teaching in an enclosed classroom without windows, you should probably not use the "blink the lights" strategy to get your students' attention. This tactic works in a classroom with a lot of windows, because you can still see your students. However, once the entire classroom goes completely dark, even for a second, any amount of silliness (or bullying) can ensue.

Do not put yourself in a situation where you could lose further control of your classroom. Examine your classroom, and try to put yourself in the mind of a young adult. If there is the potential that your "control" method could make things worse — or if it does once you employ it — try something else.

Punishment That Might Create Resentment

While I have and will continue to emphasize that trying to be your students' best friend will not help you maintain control of your classroom, there are some discipline measures that will create unnecessary resentment. The "mistakes" I detail in this section may — at times — seem like a good idea. Just make note of the possible downsides, and if you decide to employ these strategies, be aware of the potential results.

MISTAKE 37

Using group punishment…

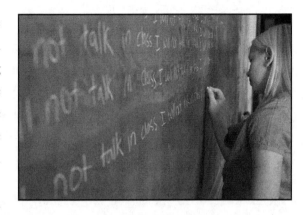

If your class starts to get rowdy or loud and you are teaching younger teens (middle school), it can be effective to use a "time out" measure that will settle the class down. These tactics could include blinking the lights in your room, telling all of your students to put their heads down for a minute, or having everyone hold up one hand while putting a finger to their lips in a "be quiet" motion.

However, beyond these "settle the class down" situations, punishing the class as a whole for the bad behavior of a couple of students will win you no respect. First, students cannot be expected to police one another, and even if teens try to leverage positive peer pressure to keep the class in line for you, it would likely fail. In fact, if a student does speak up to try to get the class to behave, they could be labeled a "teacher's pet" or "brown-noser."

Besides the fact that group punishment places the burden of creating good behavior on the students, it also creates a "you" against "them" dynamic to the classroom. While you do not necessarily need every student to love you, it should not be your goal to be seen as the children's adversary either. When you create this dichotomy to your classroom, it will make it more difficult for you to reach out to students who need help and to reward students for their achievements.

Finally, in the group punishment scenario, students will recognize that you are unable to get the few students under control who are causing the disruption. This will consciously or unconsciously lead to the students losing respect for you. Furthermore, if the students believe they will be punished anyway, rather than continuing to behave well, they might decide to join in the bad behavior of the initiators.

MISTAKE 38

Assigning extra work as punishment...

While there might be a time and place to use this strategy, generally speaking, I believe that giving extra work to the class for negative behavior of a few — or even several students — is a mistake. First, both class work and homework should be thought of as a tool for learning. Teaching your students that their work has another purpose, and a negative one at that, could undermine what you are trying to accomplish by teaching them that learning is fun.

Additionally, your students likely have a fair amount of work to get through without extra work. Assigning this type of punishment could adversely impact a student's ability to complete their assignments and get good grades. The last thing you want to do is make it harder for your students to excel in your classroom. Doing so will cause many of your students to stop caring and to stop putting in their full effort.

Finally, the extra work punishment — particularly when assigned to the entire class — has all of the downsides of the group punishment mistake. You will do more to earn your students' respect if you show them you can deal with disruptive students and minor interruptions without punishing the innocent in the process.

The one exception to this policy is not really when you need to assign "extra" work, but if the class has been derailed enough, the class work might need to become homework. Your students are less likely to see this as a punishment and more as a result of the classroom disruptions. While they might believe you should get the rowdy students in line so they do not have to do their work at home, they will understand that they are not being asked to do anything above and beyond what you already had planned for them.

MISTAKE 39

Forgetting to reward good behavior...

While you need to have a discipline plan in place and be prepared to use it to maintain control of your classroom, do not forget that one of the best ways to encourage good behavior is to recognize it, point it out to the class, and reward it.

You need to take care not to call any one student out too much in order to avoid the appearance of favoritism, but all of your students will exhibit good behavior at one time or another. Even your most disruptive child will do something you can praise if you look for it. Take those moments to reward the child for their good behavior, and reinforce the idea that they can receive attention for being good — not just being a clown.

Try to remember that children and teens are disruptive for a whole host of reasons. You do not necessarily need to identify the motivating factor behind a student's misbehavior, but do remember to use the "carrot" along with the "stick." When you praise a child who normally only gets noticed for acting out, you might see them trying to earn your attention with a positive action instead of negative one. If successful, this tactic could go a long way in turning around your student's school performance and your overall classroom management.

CHAPTER 5
Managing Distractions

Many things can prove distracting for middle and high school students — so much so that you might often wonder if your whole class is suffering from ADHD. If you thought that all you would have to do is instruct students on your subject area, then someone lied to you. You will have the privilege of wearing almost as many hats as a parent.

You will, at times, have to deal with personality conflicts among your students, be watchful and prevent bullying, and support children who are friendless. You will also need to ensure a child/teen is not mocked or teased for being poor. Finally, you will need to prevent anything in your classroom from becoming a popularity contest. This is quite a lot of social maneuvering for a teacher to pull off while trying to communicate the day's lesson. But if you do not fulfill these duties, then some students will get left behind academically.

You might be thinking, *"I did not become a teacher to be a social director or a matchmaker or any other such nonsense."* Of course, you are correct in these regards, but if you are unwilling to dedicate some of your time to monitoring the distractions that come from how your students relate to one another, you might not be able to maintain the order and structure your students need to thrive. Bullying, teasing, and other petty relationship problems do not remain in the hall when the students walk through your door — they impact your classroom as well. Be alert.

In addition to distractions that can occur in how students relate to one another, you may have to deal with distractions that come from high-tech devices such as phones, tablets, and gaming devices. If you are a recent graduate from college, then you will likely come from a world where you carry a smart phone and/or tablet on you at all times. You probably used it during your college classes and thought nothing of it — perhaps you even had a cell phone in your backpack in high school. Students having high-tech devices might not even faze you like it does others. I can assure you that if your school has a policy regarding these devices, you should enforce it strictly. If you do not, then you should make a classroom policy for yourself and not waver from it.

Your classroom is not a place for smart phones or tablets. If your students have and carry these devices, you should ensure they keep them secured and do not bring them out during your class. Below are stories, advice and recommendations regarding dealing with distractions in the classroom.

Best Friends Forever and Worst Enemies

Greeting cards and television commercials show you how cute it is when a little girl decides that a little boy is going to be her boyfriend. What these mediums fail to do is talk about the results of such "relationships" coming to an end. Tears, teasing, and fighting are hardly something you want to spill over into your classroom. While you cannot prevent such things from happening, you can make it clear to your students that whether they like or hate each other, they will respect each other and treat each other with kindness in your classroom.

Respect is an important concept to teach students of any age and goes way beyond being polite or having manners. Treating others with respect means not going through each other's stuff, not talking behind each other's back, and not teasing each other about what they are wearing or answering a question wrong in class. It is important that you lead by example, because your students will take their cues from you. Below are a few ways to avoid having "best friends" and "worst enemies" disrupt your classroom.

MISTAKE 40
Letting popularity matter in the classroom…

I cannot emphasis enough how much you should avoid letting popularity become a factor in your classroom. Allowing students to learn and practice the concept of voting is admirable, but I do not feel like middle and high school students can vote on a representative with any practical reasoning. Your school will have plenty of opportunities for students to have these experiences — Homecoming, Class Government, Prom, etc… — so there is no reason for you to bring this into your classroom and distract your students from their academic pursuits.

Instead, if you want to teach concepts of voting and majority rule, allow your children the choice between two options, and let the class vote to select one over the other. This can be a vote on which book to read or the subject of a class essay. As long as you are allowing students to vote between two possibilities, but not two people, you are limiting the popularity contest between individual students.

As you limit these instances for students, keep in mind that you should not show favoritism yourself — not to the students or parents of your students. Furthermore, you should not seek your own popularity in the school or with the students. When you become overly concerned about how well you are liked by students or staff in comparison to other teachers, you will hinder your work.

MISTAKE 41

Permitting "innocent" teasing...

Most schools proclaim loudly and frequently that they have a "zero-tolerance" policy when it comes to bullying. You are probably ready to address bullying whenever and wherever you see it. Yet, there is teasing that might not qualify as bullying but still should not be permitted in your classroom. You might even have to find yourself making sure you do not engage in it.

Children are often sensitive about things that make them standout. While you might have a few students whose parents have successfully taught them to love the things about themselves that make them unique, you will have many more students who are sensitive about silly things like having freckles, wearing glasses, or needing braces. You need to ensure that you do not overlook teasing about "little" things because they seem trivial to you.

Many teachers have wet wipes, hand sanitizer, and other such items in their classrooms regularly these days. You might want to also consider having things like deodorant or mouthwash on hand. Remaining fully stocked with these supplies will help you pull some students aside who might need to wash up a bit or deal with bad breath to help them not be embarrassed in front of their classmates. This is a difficult issue to address, and you will need to find a way to do it that will not humiliate the child, but letting students know you have these things available for them could help a student overcome needless teasing.

Other areas where you feel teasing might be "innocent" could come from students snickering about an answer a student gives in class or students teasing a child about liking something other students think is "stupid" or "childish." While these are not examples of bullying, you should encourage students to feel comfortable answering questions in your classroom. It can just take one wrong response for a student to clam up and not want to talk anymore. So, while there are "stupid" answers, do not ever let a student feel like he or she gave one. Find something in his or her answer that you can use to move them in the right direction of the lesson, and silence students who start to laugh or tease a student for giving a wrong answer quickly.

When it comes to likes and dislikes, children advance through different stages at different ages. You might have a seven-year-old who still likes Thomas the Train and one who is already into super heroes. You should not allow your student to make their classmates feel childish or wrong because of their natural likes or dislikes. This may come up as part of class discussion or aside from it. Encourage your students to be respectful of each other, and this will help you maintain a classroom where each child feels free to express themselves and participate in your learning exercises.

MISTAKE 42

Letting fights or bickering impact the classroom...

One of the things that's been most surprising for me raising a daughter is how early girls can get into "cat fights." I simply do not recall such problems when I was young. Of course, boys can get into playground scuffles and have their own version of "cattiness" as well. While this is going to happen in school, you must do what you can to prevent it from carrying over into your classroom.

It is fine if two or more of your students are upset with each other as long as they do not express it while you are teaching a lesson. If you need to separate students, then do so. I do not think you need to keep children/teens in their assigned seating and expect them to behave when ill feelings are forming between them. A little space might just help you keep your classroom under control.

Of course, if students make faces at one another and try to rile each other up every time you turn around, you might need to send them to the principal's office. If that happens, make sure you send both students so the issue can be dealt with fairly. Go ahead and admit to yourself that there are things you might have missed so that even if one child appears to be the instigator and another the victim, the principal can hear both sides of the story.

The important thing is that you do not allow a temporary or even long-lasting fight or disagreement between two or more of your students to have an impact on your classroom. Ensure that students understand that they need to respect each other and get along, or there will be negative consequences for all involved — this is one way to motivate students to make the extra effort to settle down.

MISTAKE 43

Trying to settle a student squabble or restore a broken friendship...

While you need to make sure an argument does not get out of hand (and you can lecture both students on issues such as respect and kindness), you should not attempt to solve the fight itself. Students who hate each other one week will once again be best friends the next, and they will do this on their own without any adult intervention. Your job is to ensure that your classroom is not negatively impacted while these pendulum swings occur.

In most cases, you will not need to listen to detailed stories about why one child no longer likes another. You might need to intervene if a child messed with another child's property, but you do not have to be a relationship counselor to seven-year-olds. They can often work it out on their own. Intervening anymore than necessary to maintain a healthy learning environment could exaggerate how much a distraction the squabbling proves to be — both for you and the students.

MISTAKE 44

Taking sides…

Do not ever take sides — even if you really want to, even if you believe one child is completely right and another is completely wrong. When students come to you with a problem, listen to them and consult with your supervisor or the school principal on how to handle the situation. If you immediately appear to take a side in the situation, you can be accused of bias or favoritism. In order to successfully resolve conflict, you must avoid such appearances.

Enlisting a third-party to help resolve conflict between students in your classroom is probably the best way to go. While you could serve as an arbitrator between your students, and since you need to maintain classroom order, having one or both of them think you are unfair and favor the other student will not help you. Instead, seek help and support from the staff around you, and make your main focus maintaining classroom order, not telling the children which one of them is right and which one is wrong.

MISTAKE 45

Not recognizing and stopping bullying…

Every time you hear an adult talk about how they were bullied as a child, it seems like that behavior was so blatant that some adult — some teacher — should have observed the behavior and done something about it. It is almost impossible to believe that bullying behavior always exists in a bubble where surrounding adults remain blissfully unaware. Yet it is equally difficult to imagine an adult witnessing bullying and doing nothing about it.

The lesson you need to take from this is to be observant of students in the halls, lunchrooms, and as they get on and off buses. Do not just watch your students in your classroom: watch them everywhere. You could be teaching ninth graders and see nothing amiss, but your students might be being bullied by seniors when they go to the bathroom.

If you see bullying, handle it according to your school's policy. Do not turn around and walk the other way or think some other teacher will handle it. There are things you can stay out of, like campus politics, as a new teacher, but not wanting to be confrontational when one child is bullying another is not a luxury you have — even in your first year of teaching.

High-Tech Distractions

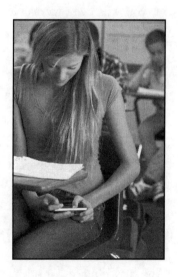

As much as student interactions with each other can cause children to be distracted from the learning process, items from home can cause the same problems. In middle and high school, the most common source of this distraction will likely be phones, tablets, and music devices. If your school is lax in this area, you might want to develop a strict classroom policy yourself, communicate it to all students and parents, and be prepared to back it up.

Technology is wonderful and can, at times, greatly aid the learning experience. In fact, you can use high-tech devices to engage your students, but this practice should be in your control and under your supervision. Anything that falls outside of those parameters is more likely to cause problems than advance the learning process.

MISTAKE 46

Allowing phones and other devices in your classroom…

My personal opinion regarding phones and high-tech devices is that students do not need to bring them to your class. If they want to have them at school, they should be kept secured in the student's locker. However, not all schools have a locker for every student and many teens might want to keep devices on their person. If this is the case, these devises should be set to silent and not brought out during your class.

Your school might have a firm policy regarding high-tech devices. If that is the case, just enforce the school's rules. If you are allowed some leniency in, you will need to decide how much responsibility you are willing to shoulder in your classroom if you permit such devices.

There are a few things I believe you should consider if you decide to allow phones and high-tech devices in your classroom. First is the cost of such items if they are lost or damaged. You might consider this solely the responsibility of the parent and teen, but you could well be put in the situation where a parent expects to hold you accountable for stolen or damaged property. Regardless of how such an issue is resolved, it puts you in a situation that would be uncomfortable at any point in your teaching career, let alone your first year.

Another thing to consider is how secure your student's possessions are in your classroom. If your students sit and remain at assigned desks during your entire class, there might be no threat of theft. However, if you teach science and your students leave their desks to sit at a lab station, their possessions might become less secure.

Finally, you should consider what the benefit of having the device is versus the potential negative that could come from having it in your classroom. If the cost outweighs the benefit, adopt a policy accordingly. If you feel the benefit is worth a little bit of risk, adopt a policy that accounts for and seeks to minimize risk as much as possible.

MISTAKE 47

Not confiscating items you do not allow in your classroom...

If you have decided that an item is not allowed in your classroom, you must be willing to confiscate it if a student brings it out and uses it. Telling the student to put the device away might solve the problem, but there are times when you are going to have to resolve a situation by taking something away from the teen.

It is better that you determine how to do this and communicate the process ahead of time to your students. That way, you can prevent the child from becoming angry or even scared that you are not going to return the item to them later. If you do not have a policy in place, then what was a distraction might turn your classroom upside down if the child overreacts.

Not being willing to take a device away in order to avoid such a reaction is not a good policy either. There are going to be times when it is necessary to confiscate something. Be prepared for it to happen, and you will avoid future headaches.

MISTAKE 48

Not making your policy clear to parents and asking for their help in enforcing your rules...

Pretty much any rule you make for your classroom needs to be understood and acknowledged by the parents of your students. This is particularly true when it comes to phones and other devices. Whatever your policy is, parents need to understand and become an active participant in reinforcing it on their end.

More importantly, though, you need parents to be aware of your policy so that if you have to enforce a punishment, then they will not be upset or angry with you. If your policy is that a parent needs to come pick up any device that is confiscated, that is something they need to know well in advance so it does not come as a surprise when it happens.

There is nothing wrong with having strict classroom rules. You just need to make sure parents are aware of these rules so they become your partner in the process. As always, active communication is the key to building successful relationships with parents.

Classroom Emergencies

The distractions that come from classroom "emergencies" can run the gambit from violence to fire drills to bomb threats. In some cases, you can manage the emergency so that it does not distract too heavily from your class. In the more serious instances, you can only manage the emergency well and maintain order while you lead your students through the situation. No matter how light or severe the emergency might be, there are a number of mistakes you should avoid.

MISTAKE 49

Not knowing what to do when a fight erupts...

Even if you work in a private school, you may run into a violent situation in your classroom. If this does happen, and a fight breaks out under your supervision, what do you do? The first thing to keep in mind is that students that have downtime are more likely to fight. Keep this empty time to a minimum by always engaging your students with something to be doing. If they are mentally involved in your lesson plan, they will not be festering over whatever it is that could be causing the fight.

If a fight does erupt, the first thing you should do is command your authority by standing up and firmly demanding that the students stop immediately. If this does not work, you should immediately call for help and have another teacher and/or administer assist you in breaking up the fight.

Never jump in the middle of the fight alone unless you are convinced you will not be seriously hurt. The last thing you need is to walk away from work with a black eye, no matter how much you want to protect your students. If you see any kind of weapon, immediately call the police.

MISTAKE 50

Not dealing with a student's vomiting in a professional manner…

The sight and sound of a person vomiting is enough to make me gag, so I do not envy the teacher who has to handle a child getting sick to their stomach at school. However, it is important that you deal with such accidents without freaking out.

If a student approaches you about having an upset stomach, you should send them to the bathroom first and then to the school nurse/office. As you get to know your students better as the year progresses, you will be able to tell which child gets butterflies before a test and which student is likely to vomit if they say they do not feel well. Until such time, err on the side of caution, and save yourself the clean up.

MISTAKE 51

Not knowing exactly what to do in case of a fire drill, bomb threats, etc…

Whether your school is having a routine fire drill or an unexpected tornado warning or bomb threat, you need to know exactly what your students need to do in all situations. Students will look to you in all situations, and you do not want your experience with a routine fire drill to look like an early scene from the movie Kindergarten Cop.

Familiarize yourself with all of your school's standard operating procedures when it comes to emergency situations, know where to take your children, and communicate to your children what they need to do in each instance.

Boredom

Perhaps there is little more distracting to a teen than being bored. There are up and down sides to living in the technology era. It seems like people are more accustomed to being electronically stimulated than ever before. Therefore, having to sit still while waiting for classmates to finish an assignment or test could be enough to make a student fidget or misbehave.

Your job is not to constantly entertain your students, but you should try to minimize the possible negative impact boredom can have on your classroom. However, in doing this, I caution you to be aware of how you could deemphasize the importance of a test in the process. Read on for examples of mistakes to avoid when combating boredom.

MISTAKE 52

Assigning too much work...

In researching this book, I came across the concept that you should not allow children to sit around with nothing important to do at any point in time. I realize that this seems like good advice since you have a lot of material to cover and you need to make sure your students grasp it all before the year is through. But there is such a thing as information overload.

In most schools across the country, students are getting less and less playtime outside. There is a ton of research that validates the premise that outside play and exercise benefit the learning process, but schools just do not have time to fit it in anymore. While this may be your problem, there is little you can do to correct it. Instead, you have to work around it.

However, I do not believe the best way to work around children getting bored or fidgety is to just assign more work. First, some children need more time to complete work than others, and they should not feel pressure to finish because other students have started on something else. Next, when a student has completed a hard test or assignment, it could be helpful to let them relax for a few minutes and recoup for the next class of the day. Handing them more work — particularly if it is just "busy" work — robs them of the chance to have some downtime.

Set a reasonable goal for how much work you can get through in a day or week, and allow yourself some room for if the class goes faster or slower than expected. If you find your students need more time on a portion of your curriculum, slow down and go over the material again. If you run through some subject matter quickly, have a learning activity planned that will reinforce what you are teaching but also lets the students have a little fun.

Or you can reward your children with a little "free" time while you sit at your desk and do some work. If this scares you, remember that not every minute of a student's day needs to be scheduled. Allow your students a little time to study, work ahead on homework, or read gives them a little bit of flexibility in an otherwise very structured environment. If the class starts to get unruly, you will need to step in, but you might find that they can handle a little free time and still behave well.

MISTAKE 53
Not using hands-on work...

You probably do not want to have your students dancing around your classroom all too often, so you may not be able to give them the physical outlet they need on days when they get restless. However, you can be sure to engage them in plenty of hands-on or demonstrative activities. "Once a teacher brought in cupcakes and straws to explain a science concept to us," explained Brandy Mayer. "When she put the straw into the center of the cupcake for a sample, it came out with different layers of filling. I liked it when teachers were creative like that."

You do not need to run out and become a master baker, but using a few hands-on activities to demonstrate science or math principals may help engage your students in a subject they otherwise find boring. Also, try to remember that young children learn very well with their hands. As a result, puzzles or other learning games that involve assembling things can be an effective way for some students to master a lesson.

MISTAKE 54

Just having your students sit quietly and read their textbook…

While a little planned downtime can be beneficial to your students, having days when you just have them sit and read their textbooks is not a good way to keep them engaged in the subject matter. Students expect you to teach them and lead the class in some way. If you tell them to just sit and read their textbooks in silence, there is a chance they will begin to pass notes, whisper, or do something other than what you asked them.

If you want to allow your students some time to read in class so that they do not have to do all of their reading at home, you should at least host a discussion period after 20 or 30 minutes of reading. That way, you can ask your students questions and encourage them to ask you about material they did not understand. By scheduling reading sessions in this manner, you can be sure your students comprehend what they are reading and you have a plan in place that you can employ if they appear to be getting bored or restless.

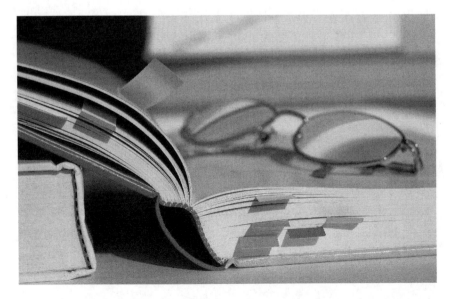

School-Scheduled Distractions

Believe it or not, some things that cause distractions in your class will actually be caused by the school itself. You will probably be made aware of testing ahead of time and be able to schedule around those little standardized distractions. However, there will also be fire drills, school plays, class pictures, and other interruptions that can take you off course.

> **MISTAKE 55**
>
> ## Not having a back-up plan for interruptions...
>
> "Make a separate notebook for emergency plans to be used when there are things that are messing up your day," advises retired history teacher and department head Bill Hayes. "Also, put materials in folders that can be used if you ever have to be out."
>
> Having a back-up plan in place will help you maintain control of your classroom even as chaos seems to rule the day, and it will help you make good use of your time even if you have to abandon your original lesson plan.

CHAPTER 6
Overcoming Challenges to Learning

As a teacher, you are going to see all kinds of students, which means you are going to become familiar with all kinds of learning challenges. Some challenges are internal to the student (such as having a lack of motivation), while others are external factors (such as having a student that has an insane schedule).

It is not your job to solve all of your student's problems, no matter how much you might want to; you probably will not be able to be their hero. However, you can recognize if these challenges are affecting a child's work, and you can try to help the student overcome whatever issues or challenges they are facing.

MISTAKE 56

Not knowing how to deal with students who have no motivation…

This is going to be a problem that you will face at one point or another, and it might even be with multiple students at once. It might be a core issue — an issue that is across the board. For example, you may come across a student that never does his homework, that is always late to class, and that is sleeping at every given opportunity.

On the other hand, you may come across a student that has a lack of motivation for a more concentrated reason — they are not interested in the material you are teaching. Perhaps they cannot see what value this material will ever have for their future (we have all been there, have we not?).

If you have a student that is completely devoid of motivation, that might be a situation that is better suited for a guidance counselor or psychologist, and you should do your best to set up an initial meeting. However, if you have a student that is experiencing a lack of motivation because she is not interested in today's lesson, there are things you can do.

You need to do your best to make your lessons as engaging and as inspiring as humanly possible. Even if you are teaching your students about how paint dries, it is your duty to catch their interest in one way or another. Perhaps you can use multimedia components, interesting and modern examples for outdated history lessons, or even a story to get them interested. No matter how dry the content in the lesson can be, your job as a teacher is to interest your students and make the material relevant.

Whatever you do, do not just assign a chapter of reading to your students. Nothing is more irrelevant and boring than reading a chapter from a textbook (well, maybe some things are), but the point is that they need you to do your magic and spark their motivation so that they can be immersed in whatever the subject may be.

MISTAKE 57
Not knowing how to deal with students who have a busy schedule…

It is never your job to cater to a student who is in many extracurricular activities. However, you do need to know how to deal with these students when the situation arises.

How you deal with the situation heavily relies on the individual student, but here is an example. Let us say that you have a student involved in basketball, choir, band, and dance lessons. She has a game, a choir rehearsal, a band rehearsal, and her ballet lesson all within a two-day period, and these are conveniently the same days you had your big exam planned.

It can be tempting to offer this student an extension or additional help, but remember that she willingly took on all of these activities — life cannot always cater to the schedule of your students. As adults, we all know that if we start to get overwhelmed, the first thing we should do is see what kinds of commitments we can cut out in order to release some stress. If you do not let your students learn this lesson now, you are doing them a disservice.

You may also come across students who must miss huge chunks of school for varying reasons — for example, you might have a celebrity student who must leave school to do some type of work. You may be thinking that this is the most irrelevant thing you have ever heard, but it does happen, and we are covering all the bases here, right?

Take the rapper, Drake, for example, who dropped out of high school to act on the hit TV series *Degrassi: The Next Generation*. He made the decision to drop out in order to balance his life — he could not keep going to school while also making time to act on the show. (He did end up graduating from high school at the age of 25.) Whatever the situation may be, this is a decision your students must make — not you.

In order to determine the best course of action for the student, you might need to consult with the teen's parents, other teachers, and school resources, such as counselors. Let them know if the student is falling behind because of too many commitments, and make it clear that you cannot be constantly extending deadlines or giving special treatment to any one student.

MISTAKE 58

Not knowing how to deal with students who are not tech-savvy...

While many youngsters are surprisingly amazing at figuring out technology, this is not always going to be the case. If you are utilizing technology in your classroom, you need to be conscious of how tech-savvy your students are. Do not let a student become embarrassed if he has no clue how to use a word processing program or even an online search engine.

You will come across students who do not own a computer at home, so be careful when you think about assigning homework that requires Internet use or the use of a printer. Make sure to give your students plenty of time to make arrangements to use the school's computers to get these things done.

If you ever have a lesson that requires the use of technology, make sure you explain every step with extreme detail — pretend you are instructing elementary-aged students, not teens. This can help to ease the nerves of students who might quickly become lost, thus falling behind and possibly becoming too embarrassed to admit their total confusion.

If you have an assignment that requires the use of a more complicated program or type of software, make sure you provide your students with learning material, such as links to online tutorials or even a list of steps. The most important thing is that you are helping your students learn, not embarrassing them for their lack of knowledge.

MISTAKE 59

Not knowing how to deal with students who cannot handle criticism…

You are going to come across students that seem incapable of handling criticism. Your students are learning, and it is your job to teach them how to handle it.

There will always be the struggle between the desire to effectively teach your students and the desire to protect them from hurt feelings. However, you can do your best to bridge the gap by following these general tips:

Carefully monitor your body language. When you are giving a student negative feedback on something they have turned in, it is important to remember that they are picking up on your body language as well as your words. If you cross your arms, are towering over them, or have a tense face, they will pick up on these nonverbal cues and your tense mood. In general, keep your arms comfortably at your sides, do your best to be at their eye-level, and give them the feedback with a smile.

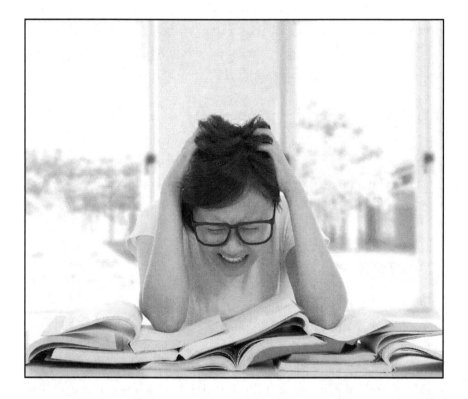

Give feedback as often as possible. If you have never given feedback before and suddenly drop a bomb on a student, it will be painful regardless of whether your arms or crossed or not. It is important to make this a regular occurrence so that your students expect it and become accustomed to the criticism. You will find that your students will be more comfortable when hearing the feedback if you make sure it happens often.

Do not always praise your students. When you constantly praise your students for a job well-done, it can actually turn into a negative thing. Your students might start to become discouraged about taking on new challenges. It can also harm their self-esteem, believe it or not. You want to make sure your students get used to hearing constructive criticism.

Do not leave your student high and dry. Once you give your student the bad news, the worst thing you can do is to excuse them from your presence. They are most likely a little bummed, so it is important that you work with him to come up with a new plan. Help your student come up with some goals or a new plan of action, but make sure that the student comes up with it, not you.

The best way to do this is by asking questions: "What can you do differently to solve the issue?" or "How do you think you could make this assignment go from average to spectacular?"

Know what to expect. When most students experience criticism, they are either going to get defensive or they are going to completely shut down on you. You need to make sure that they know how valuable criticism is. Turn it into a positive lesson, not a negative one. Make sure they know that the criticism is not about them as a person, but it is about their work. They should know that it is not a personal attack by any stretch of the imagination.

This can be a tough part of teaching, but it is your job to make sure that students are living up to their potential. You might be surprised how far students can push themselves if you start giving them valuable criticism.

CHAPTER 7
Teaching Children Through Puberty

It is very important that your expectations of the children/teens match up with their ages and capabilities. You neither want to be overly harsh or demanding nor have too low of expectations. As middle and high school teachers, you might be elated that you have avoided some of the more mundane work elementary-aged teachers have to trudge through.

However, you will have to accept and come up with ways to deal with the fact that you are teaching students through what very well might be the most difficult period of their life. From the 12 and 13-year-olds in 7th grade to the 17 and 18-year-olds about to graduate high school, hormones will rage, bodies will change, and young boys and girls will become adults before your very eyes.

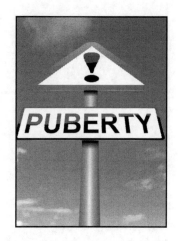

The challenges of puberty are different at every age, but you can expect embarrassment and physical changes, the ups and downs of first loves, and even the results of sexual encounters to spill over into your classroom. While this is not a foolproof list, read on for mistakes to avoid when teaching children through this awkward period of life.

MISTAKE 60

Not understanding that girl's periods can come without warning…

In middle school and even high school, a girl's period is far from the code phrase of "her friend visiting" and can often seem like her worst enemy. Her first period — and many of the ones that follow — can come without warning. She might not experience bloating, cramping, or any other signs to let her know she needs to prepare for her period to start and can therefore be caught unaware at school.

If your school is the kind that sells tampons and pads in the student bathrooms, then a girl might be able to deal with this situation rather easily. However, it might not be a bad idea for a female teacher to keep some of these items in her desk should a student need to come to her. Additionally, if a student should start her period and bleed through in such a way that it is noticeable on her clothing, she should be allowed to call her parents for a change of clothes. If you can help her by allowing her to use your phone rather than sending her to the office, do so.

It is always important to avoid the appearance of favoritism with students, but you can balance that with the need to help students avoid humiliation when possible.

MISTAKE 61

Commenting on changes the students are experiencing...

When a boy's voice cracks or he starts to grow a mustache, it might be tempting to blurt out something in front of the class. This should be avoided when possible. Students embarrass easily, and since teasing is something you want to avoid in your classroom, as little attention should be paid to puberty as possible.

If you think a student's parent needs to be made aware of his or her developmental changes, such as a boy's need to shave or a girl's need to wear a bra, then you can contact the parent and schedule a meeting. You can also ask your school's guidance counselor to talk to the student if you think it is necessary.

MISTAKE 62

Permitting sexual harassment...

As student's bodies are changing, they are becoming increasingly aware of their sexual urges and desires. While it is not your place to prevent them from having sex, it is your duty to ensure your classroom is free of sexual harassment from both genders.

Neither your female nor your male students should be made to feel as if they are receiving unwanted sexual attention while at school. You need to be mindful of how students interact and respond to one another. If a boy or girl seems like they are uncomfortable with how another student is talking or flirting with them, you might need to separate those students.

Reminding students that they need to focus on their class work is productive, but you need to ensure that their learning environment is conducive for them to do so. Make sure your students know that you expect them to respect one another and that you will not tolerate harassing behavior or displays of affection — wanted or not.

MISTAKE 63
Flirting with students…

Many people in their 20's have what I would call a flirtatious personality. Without meaning to, men and women in this age group could flirt with a bowl of rice. As a teacher, you need to be mindful of the signals you could be sending to students with your smile, laugh, or even touch. You want to be sure you are not implying a level of intimacy that does not exist or a desire for a relationship that could get your arrested, fired, or both.

PART TWO

RELATIONSHIPS

You might be wondering why a book about teaching mistakes would dedicate a large section of its pages to relationships. After all, why do relationships matter in a school setting?

Simply put, how well you relate to your students, their parents, and even your colleagues will matter as much to your career as how well you develop knowledge and skills in your students. Even as you treat your students in an egalitarian manner, you will still form unique relationships with each child, because every child is different. One student might take away from your class a love for science, while another student will always remember you as the teacher that helped them finally master their times tables. The different things your students remember you for will be as varied as the reasons you remember them.

Furthermore, you will form on varying levels relationships with your students' parents. Perhaps that relationship will amount to little more than a few teacher conferences a year to go over grades. Or you could get to know the parents of a child very well as you seek to help them deal with a learning disability. Whether you interact with a parent a little or a great deal, relating to them in an effective manner will make your teaching efforts more successful.

These two sets of relationships — parents and students — are vital to your success as a teacher. To optimize your professional achievements, there is one other relationship you should foster as much as possible — the one you hold with your colleagues and administration. Not only can other teachers help you and guide you in handling a difficult situation with a child or parent, but they can also help you to advance your career. Getting involved in your school at a level you can handle without burning out can help move you from "new kid" to "valued employee" over the course of your first year of teaching. Ignoring these relationships could hurt you when hiring and retention decisions need to be made.

CHAPTER 8
Curriculum Strategies

I wish I could tell you that if you can manage your classroom well then teaching will be easy as pie. I also wish I could tell you that the coursework you covered while completing your degree prepared you for every situation. The truth is that there are several challenges you will face during developing and communicating course material to your students; you might be aware of some challenges, and others could come as a surprise.

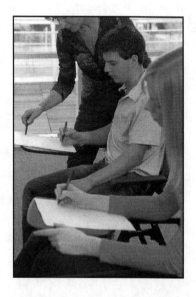

These challenges include trying to achieve the balance between creative/blended learning methodologies and preparing students for standardized tests. You could face difficulty in finding ways to engage bored students, challenging advanced students, or not getting frustrated when students fail to quickly grasp the material you are trying to teach.

Developing curriculum that will teach your students all the lessons they need to fulfill academic standards for their grade level might seem fairly straightforward at a first glance. However, using visual, audible, and hands-on learning techniques while keeping yourself flexible so that you can speed up or slow down as needed, might not be very easy to do in your first year of teaching.

Even though you are the teacher and have prepared yourself for years to teach, you still have much to learn, and you will learn new things each year as each new group of students comes in. You have to learn about your students, what they know, what they need help in, their strengths and weaknesses, what engages and makes them love learning, and even more. In order to make the most of the school year, you must learn these things about your students early while remaining flexible as new discoveries are made throughout the year. Please review the following mistakes, and see what lessons you can learn from them.

MISTAKE 64

Teaching just so students do well on standardized tests...

In states such as Florida, the idea of "teaching for tests" has become the bane of teachers everywhere. The instinct of legislatures wanting to measure the success of teachers or schools makes some sense, but the execution of tying school funding to test results has created an atmosphere where students feel tremendous pressure to do well on tests, and teachers feel like they must prepare children to achieve results that will get them ranked as an 'A' school.

While legislative policies cannot be changed easily, this book addresses why falling into the trap of "teaching for tests" will do you little good during your first year of teaching (or ever). If you fall into the category of teaching that is measured by state tests, you might feel a great deal of pressure to make sure your students can do well on these exams — but ignore it.

This might sound extreme to suggest that you should ignore this impulse because, of course, these test results are important, but I can assure you that teaching strictly for these tests will not make your students more prepared than if you just cover material in a natural manner that works for your classroom.

Throughout the year, you will have to introduce your students to the process of standardized testing, such as not talking while taking tests and filling in answer forms properly, but you can work that into a normal testing scenario. You can even make learning to fill in answer forms a classroom or homework activity where the purpose is to color in the bubbles fully and neatly — not to answer hard questions.

Approach standardized testing with the mindset that it should just be an evaluation of your teaching, not the point of your teaching. You can instruct your students about all the materials they need to learn without boring them or making them feel more pressure than what is necessary for the testing process. Furthermore, you will feel better about going to work each day, which can only enhance the learning experience for your students.

MISTAKE 65

Teaching as if tests do not matter…

As much as I just said that you should not teach for tests, you cannot ignore the fact that these tests have real-world implications. While you should not adjust your entire curriculum to center itself on these tests, you need to keep in mind the elements of such tests that will be different for the children in your class.

For example, while there is a decent chance your student has used a Scranton answer sheet prior to this academic year, you still might want to make sure they know how to fill it in properly. After all, an improperly coded or messy answer sheet can produce negative results even if the student knows the material. You can try to make this a fun classroom exercise or just use Scranton sheets on your own tests so you know your students are prepared when the time comes for school-wide testing.

Other ways you can prepare students for standardized testing is to implement rules early on that they will need to follow during the test. You might need to warn them that they cannot talk during tests for any reason or instruct them to sit down with a couple of sharpened No. 2 pencils so they do not have to get up during the test.

I recommend starting out lightly at the beginning of the semester to introduce these concepts — give five extra points on a test if the student is sitting at their desk with sharpened pencils ready to begin at the start of class, or deduct points if a student is caught talking or asks to go to the bathroom in the middle of a test. Then, you can strengthen the consequences of not following these rules as the semester advances.

MISTAKE 66

Being too hard on children who do not test well in this environment...

When it comes to preparing children to take standardized tests, I caution against a "zero-tolerance" policy early on, because many students might not be used to the rules that apply to this form of testing and should be given some time to get accustomed to following them.

When my daughter was in third grade, she faced a zero-tolerance policy like this at one point. I had studied her spelling list with her, and I knew she was prepared for her test. So, naturally, when she came home with a zero because of "cheating", I was very concerned.

I spoke with the teacher via email, and she explained that this had happened because my daughter had been caught talking. According to my daughter, another child had asked her a question, and she answered. Since I was completely confident that my daughter was not asking for or giving help, I asked the teacher if there was anything we could do. My daughter was allowed to take a harder version of the test and have it count for her grade — and she passed without issue like I knew she would. She was just unfamiliar with the classroom rules and needed an adjustment period. While nothing like this happened again, I still remember thinking it was harsh for the start of the school year.

Again, I believe you should place a focus on preparing students for these tests, but do so slowly and without placing more stress on the students than needed.

MISTAKE 67

Getting frustrated with students who are not grasping the material and are not ready to "move on"...

Many teachers think that once a lesson is taught, it is time to move on to the next area of study. If a student or several students are lagging behind or are not grasping the material, you might feel frustrated and tempted to move on and just let that material slide. While I understand that you have much ground to cover in a school year and are concerned about how the students will measure up if you lag too long in one area, it is best to be flexible with your curriculum.

If you are only losing ground with one or two students, then you can offer special tutoring to help those students catch up. But if students do not understand the lesson, then you need to take some extra time to communicate the lesson effectively. Perhaps you need to try to convey it in a new way or just spend more time working with each student one-on-one until most of your students catch on. Just remember, there might be times when your students move through material faster than you thought, and things will balance out.

MISTAKE 68

Ignoring bad or bored students…

As a new teacher, if you have a student who is performing badly, you might be motivated to provide them with extra help and work with them to raise their grades. That is an excellent instinct, and many sections of this book will address how to do that.

However, on the opposite end of the spectrum, if you have a student who has a bad reputation or is acting disinterested in your instruction, you might be inclined to leave them alone after a while. I want to caution you against giving up on such students; even a little effort can go a long way to get a child to pay attention in class.

Christian Langley, a current stay-at-home dad, taught high school history for several years and recently told me about an experience he had with one particular student who was performing poorly. Chris said he was sitting in a parent-teacher conference listening to the other teachers, and when it was his turn to talk, he had to say that his experience with the student was not the same. He said the student was not an A student, but he performed well enough to earn a solid C in his class.

Chris told me that one of the biggest differences he noted between himself and some of the other teachers was that he would get up and walk around the room when the students were working silently at their desks or taking tests or even during his lectures. He said that it is surprising how well a student will wake themselves up and focus when you stand beside their desk for a few minutes.

I believe the lesson behind this is that you can engage your less-inclined students as well as your best performing ones. It is okay to call upon a student who you suspect is too scared to participate in class or create activities that all students can contribute to. Get up, walk around your room, and ask the students if they have any questions individually. These small steps can encourage participation and develop a relationship needed to help a bad student turn things around.

MISTAKE 69
Not engaging students who are more advanced…

On the opposite end of the spectrum are advanced children who might not need your help at all. Even if you do not teach advanced classes, you will likely have some superstars in your classroom that eagerly soak up all of the knowledge you have to impart of him or her. These students will get almost everything right, raise their hand to answer questions, finish their work without your help, and just be really easy for you to handle.

You will likely consider such students heaven-sent during the hardest lessons you have to teach, but do not make the mistake of ignoring these students and not challenging them. As the mother of a daughter who can be restless in the classroom and a son who is overly talkative, I know how important it is for teachers to keep good students occupied even while they seek to work with slower ones.

Just remember that while you want to recognize good work, you need to avoid the appearance of favoritism. Seek to balance the efforts you make between keeping advanced students busy and engaged without having a "teacher's pet." Finally, if you believe these students are advanced enough to be in an honors or gifted class the following year, be sure to recommend testing or placement. Read the next section to see why.

MISTAKE 70

Not recognizing when a student needs to be challenged more…

At times, the difference between a well-behaved and a poorly-behaved student is a matter of engagement and challenge. Other times, recognizing a teen's potential could set them on the path that will lead them to their future career. No matter what, it is important that you observe your students, their needs, and their responses to work so you can help shape their academic schedules and pursuits the following year.

If you are teaching a basic-level course, and you start to suspect that a student could be doing higher-level work, go ahead and challenge him or her to see if you are correct. At times, the reason a student is in remedial classes is because of a lack of support at home or a tendency to get into fights or trouble with other students. If you can encourage or inspire that student to overcome their challenges and get more out of their education, you can make a real difference in their life.

On the other hand, you might have a student who is doing very well in school, but shows a strong potential in a particular subject area where they need to be more challenged. From my experience in school, students tend to get clumped into advanced, average, and remedial categories, but that is simply not how people function. Students can be better in some subject areas than others and should be encouraged to pursue advanced classes in the area where they excel.

My friend, Sigmarie Soto, a professional business and technical writer, was one such student. "In tenth grade, I was still unsure of my passions and interests. All I did know was that I was not good at math and science. My English teacher assigned us a full research paper on any novel of our choice, so I decided to go with Virginia Woolf's *Mrs. Dalloway*. When I received my graded paper, the teacher told me that I belonged in advanced placement English. He took it a step further by making sure I was placed in the advanced English class for the next year if I was interested. He was always encouraging, and I can honestly say that his actions put me on the path to getting a degree in English and writing for a living."

While you are busy and are learning everything it means to be a new teacher, remember to take the time to recognize the strengths and talents of your students, and encourage them to maximize the education they receive in these areas.

MISTAKE 71

Using words or language your students do not understand…

As a parent, I never engaged in the practice of "baby talk," and I never talked "down" to my children. However, I did encourage them to ask questions if I used words they did not understand and was ready to use a synonym to explain a word if my vocabulary exceeded their understanding.

While you want to expand your students' vocabulary — and you will undoubtedly do so over the course of the school year — you probably do not have time to stop your lesson every time one of 20+ students misses your meaning. As a result, you should try to use words your students will understand while making sure you repeatedly use the vocabulary your class might be studying that week.

CHAPTER 9
Teaching Facts, Skills, & Concepts

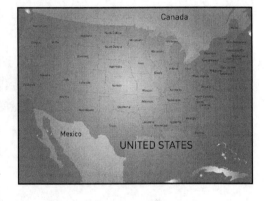

When teaching middle school and high school students, you are not just instructing them on historical data and mathematical facts to memorize. You will be teaching them concepts and valuable skill sets as well — hopefully ones that they will carry with them during their entire academic career.

Teachers communicate many facts to their students, from rules of grammar to the year Christopher Columbus discovered the Americas. They help children memorize definitions, names, dates, formulas, the names of state capitals, and more. These facts do not require critical thinking or analysis. Children do not need to deduct anything to regurgitate these facts on tests.

I do not mean to belittle the teaching of facts. In the time I spent teaching "American Federal Government," I did quite a lot of communication of facts to the adult students in my classroom. Furthermore, my tests did require my students be able to answer questions based solely on the facts and figures they memorized over the course of the class.

However, much of teaching is not just the communication of facts. It is instructing students in a diverse set of skills, including critical thinking. Facts can be memorized, but skills must be learned and then put into practice. You cannot just memorize how to read; you must practice reading to become truly proficient. Furthermore, you must be able to analyze what you have read to learn the skill of implicit reading comprehension. Helping your students learn this skill requires more than just practice — it involves discussion, debate, and engagement.

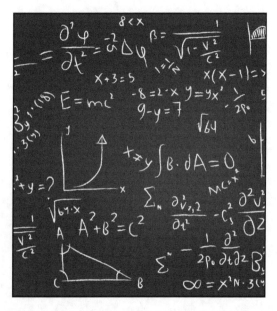

When you instruct students on concepts, you will be helping students to not only answer the "what" question of learning, but you will be tackling the ever elusive "why." I confess to being the anomaly in parenting, because I would humor the "why" question until we go to a point where I thought the explanation was beyond my child's understanding. This could be a matter of tackling a scientific concept that I was just unable to explain or at times, it could mean that we had reached a point in a car conversation where I thought visual aids would be needed to go any further. I do not know yet if my indulgence of the "why" game was beneficial to my children, but I believe that as a teacher, you will be expected to help students finally get their "why" answers.

Concepts teach students how things relate to one another or how processes work. Instructing students on photosynthesis is about more than teaching pure scientific facts — it involves showing students how nature ties together. When you instruct students on the parts of the flower and explain to them how pollinators move the process of pollination and help flowers reproduce, you are not teaching just facts to memorize. Students need to see how these concepts tie together in order to truly understand the subject matter.

This chapter is dedicated to mistakes that can be made when teaching facts, skills, and concepts to students and how to make sure your students are getting the most of each category of learning.

MISTAKE 72
Being opposed to re-teaching facts or concepts students should already know...

Students learn certain skills each year of school, and they must be proficient in certain abilities to advance to their next grade. As your students advance through middle and high school, they will start to be separated on the basis of interests and difficulty that they can handle. Some students will complete Algebra I in 8th grade, while others will take it in high school. Regardless, you can expect that students will need review at certain times of year or as you approach new ideas.

When speaking with your students at the start of the year, and you are met with nothing but blank faces when you start using words like "prime numbers" and "scientific theory," you might be tempted to throw your hands up in the air and wonder if these kids know anything at all.

After spending some time in the trenches of tutoring, I can attest that speaking to children about math facts and rules of grammar is a little like speaking to a person learning a foreign language. After taking French for two years in high school, I decided to advance my skills in college and took a couple of semesters there as well. I can still remember my Parisian French professor looking at me after a few class sessions and saying "Où habitez-vous?"

Required to speak only in French and not having any idea what she was saying, my only available response was "Je ne sais pas." This is of course my favorite French phrase, and if you cannot guess what it means, it translates to "I do not know."

Now going back to the original question the professor was asking me, it translates to "Where do you live?" Did I know where I lived? Of course I did. But despite the fact that she said the phrase several times, I could not conclude what she was asking. Interestingly, when she became a little frustrated and wrote the phrase, I was able to understand it and excitedly replied "J'habite un Etats-unis!" Not a perfect coin of phrase, but it was fairly close to "I live in the United States."

My French skills have not advanced much beyond this level, and I was always able to read and write French better than I could hold a conversation. The point of the story is that until I could see the phrase written, I was hopelessly clueless. Your students might know what you are talking about if you jog their memories a little first.

Basically, after a summer of video games, swimming pools, and super hero movies, you have to get your students once again speaking the same language you are using. So, before you make a note to speak to teachers from the grade below you, try some board exercises or visual aids. The results might be somewhat reassuring.

However, even once you get your students on the same page as you, some of them still might not remember the skills they learned the year before. If they forget, it is your job to bring their skills back up to par so you can progress them toward more advanced skill sets. Therefore, any time you tackle a new subject, be prepared to review the basics before you get into the meaty part of the lesson. If you find some students in need of extensive remediation teachings, consider offering them after school assistance.

MISTAKE 73
Not reviewing after shorter school breaks…

You may understand the importance of review material after a long summer break, but do not overlook the need to review a little after holiday breaks such as Thanksgiving, Christmas, and Spring Break. Anytime a child closes their books for a week or more, there is a least some possibility that they will forget the material you covered before break.

In fact, you can almost consider it a given that your students will not remember anything you covered prior to that break well enough to test on it. Do your best to schedule section tests prior to long student breaks. If you need to administer a test after a break, spend some time reviewing the material, and make sure they are capable of doing well.

MISTAKE 74

Expecting transfer students to be on the same page as your class...

This book is being written amidst the turmoil surrounding "Common Core" curriculum and the corresponding effort to develop a standardized teaching practice across the U.S. Concurrently, there is a rising tide to the counter argument that children learn at different speeds and trying to fit them all into one mold is quite damaging to their development.

Of course, one of the reasons the proponents for a standardized teaching curriculum arose to begin with is that from state to state, and even school to school, what a student learns can vary greatly. This creates an environment where if a student transfers into a new school, they could be lagging behind, or they could be advanced beyond their peers just because their old school moved at a different pace than their new one.

Whether or not we ever achieve a common thread in our education system between the states, teachers must simply accept that a transfer student might be at a different point than the children entering their classroom having attended the school the year before. As a result, you need to be prepared to meet that student's needs and adjust your plan a little to either catch them up to your class or keep them engaged while you cover material they already know.

MISTAKE 75

Thinking a student is slow because they are lacking a certain skill set...

Whether or not a student came from another school or just did not master a skill set they should have before coming into your classroom, you should recognize that an inability in one area does not equal a lack of ability across the board.

While most people recognize that adults are good at some things and not others, we do not necessarily recognize this fact in teens. Even when students reach the high school level, an honors or gifted student will be encouraged to take advanced courses in every subject. The simple fact is that a student might be well qualified to take advanced science, but should only be in an average-level English class.

Since this book is targeting teachers who instruct teens, my advice is to not conclude that a student will be good in everything just because they are good in some things. Nor conversely should you believe that a student is slow if they are struggling in one subject area. Try to recognize your students' strengths and weaknesses and help them where they need it while challenging them where appropriate.

MISTAKE 76

Grouping students according to ability...

On the surface, separating groups according to their demonstrated skill level might seem like a good idea. And it is true enough that we do this when we create honors or Advanced Placement classes. In fact, it is reasonable to believe that this separation will help students achieve more in areas where they excel while bringing up their weaker skills sets. A high school student might be able to take advanced language and more rudimentary math allowing them to be challenged according to their talents and capabilities.

The problem is that some research indicates this type of segregation in the classroom only benefits the stronger students without creating the "extra support" the slower students need. It is reported that teachers often have lower expectations, demands, and tolerance for the slowest groups of students, and the quality of instruction for these students decreases.

Some researchers suggest that because students possess academic strengths and weaknesses, grouping children in slow or advanced groups can lower their self-esteem unnecessarily. Instead, supplementing a child's lagging area with peer-tutoring or after-school help can allow the student to catch up in their weak skill area without the perception of being labeled "slow" or "stupid" (Mason & Good 1993).

Since as a middle or high school teacher, you will be instructing your students in a subject-specific area, be sure to use this research to ensure that you provide strong incentive to all of your students, not just the more advanced ones.

CHAPTER 10
Tests & Homework

Homework and tests are an important part of your curriculum as well as quizzes, classroom participation, presentations, book reports, and various other methods you can use to evaluate if your students have mastered the material. It is important that the means you use to assess your children's understanding of the subjects you teach is properly designed for their skill level while employing several different methodologies.

Not every student will test well. Some will do better on certain types of questions (multiple choice) than others (essay). Be sure that when you design tests and homework assignments, you make sure you are not using just one method of evaluation. Also, ensure that your methods are appropriate for the age you are teaching.

The most important thing to remember is that you can change your methods as the year progresses. If you try something, and it does not seem to work for any of the children in your classroom, be open to altering your lesson plan accordingly. Read on for a more specific discussion on both homework and testing mistakes to avoid.

The Great Homework Debate

From the time I was a child until today, there has been an interesting change in how parents schedule their child's time and how parents feel about homework. I do not know if I have been blessed with incredibly adept children or teachers who do not assign a plethora of busy work, but I have rarely had to share the sentiment I see and hear about the horrors of homework.

Furthermore, while I believe there is merit to organized sports, social events, and even extracurricular activities such as music lessons or martial arts, I do not believe that children or teens need to be over-scheduled every night of the week. I am a parent who believes that school comes first and other activities should be peppered into a child's life as academics permit. After all, school itself still offers numerous ways for students to be enriched through sports and electives — i.e. practical arts, performing arts, languages, and more — within a structured day. The options only expand as children move from middle school to high school.

I commiserate with any teachers who believe that parents are over-scheduling their children and transforming extracurricular activities into academic distractions. Still, there is research that supports the idea that homework volume has increased over time. A University of Michigan research study of thousands of school aged-children ranging from 6 to 17 reports that time spent on homework increased from 2 hours and 38 minutes to nearly 4 hours since 1981 (Hancock 2011).

The sentiment against homework and criticism of testing measures, from teaching to pass standardized tests to tests that are ill-designed for the way all students learn, is only exacerbated when a parent looks at the homework or test and finds them ill-conceived (like many opponents of the common core profess) or when parents help a child do hours of homework that's not graded but only recorded as a homework grade.

There are few things that are more frustrating than to do something that feels like it has no point. As the coach of any team will tell you, practice is vital to prepare yourself to face and overcome a challenge. Homework — or practice tests — has a place in academics, and testing is important to measure students' progress and success. However, there are mistakes you can make in creating and assigning these, and those mistakes could lead you into conflict with parents.

MISTAKE 77

Giving "busy work"...

If you do not want parents cursing your name, then do not assign homework that is just "busy" work. I understand that you believe practice work is good for students, and you probably record a homework grade if the students do their work and turn it in, but if you are too busy to correct the work, do not assign it. It is just that simple. If you find yourself just checking off work without reviewing it in class with the students, you are likely assigning work that does not need to be done, and it's probably infuriating the parents of your student in the process.

I still remember sitting down with my fiancé's oldest son and trying figure out why he was struggling with math. I was very surprised to see that he was doing his math homework wrong, and his teacher never pointed that out. His teacher was giving him a homework grade for doing the work, but not reviewing it in class or checking to see if it was done correctly. And let us face it: practicing something the wrong way is a quick path to failure.

If you practice playing football without learning the rules of the game and it comes time to play, you could find yourself unable to advance down the field due to penalties. To achieve success, you must practice following the rules as much as completing a pass or a run.

When it comes to homework, it is not enough that students do the work you give them just for a homework grade. If that homework is going to benefit the student, then it must be reviewed so the student can learn what they did wrong and how to fix it. I believe too much of homework for elementary-aged students falls into this "busy" work category, which is why students are not learning anything from the process.

My advice is to give homework that will be followed-up the next day in class and assign homework that the student was unable to complete that day. If you are teaching reading, have students read at home and discuss the passage in class. If you are teaching math, convey the lesson, do some practice problems together, let the students do the work at home, and then review it together the next day. If you have students write sentences at home for spelling or vocabulary words, assign your students to read and share them in class to vote on which ones were used the best.

Remember that as important as your time is, you do not want to overwhelm yourself with grading; students and parents need to feel like their time is not being wasted either. All homework assignments should have meaning and value. If it is nothing more than a check mark, you and the students can probably do without it.

MISTAKE 78

Giving too much homework…

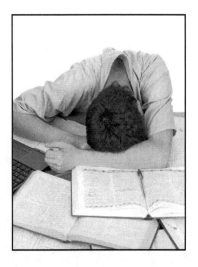

Once students enter middle school/high school and have different teachers for their core subjects, the simple truth is that you are going to end up with an overload of homework one night or another or all your tests scheduled on the same day. A middle school and high school student has to plan ahead, work hard, study, and learn valuable organizational and time-management skills along the way.

However, in order to ensure that you are giving your students their best chance at success, make sure that you are not giving too much homework for your individual class. Consult other teachers and see how much work they assign, and if you get a chance, make note of when other instructors assign their bigger projects so you can schedule yours at a different time.

While teens are often convinced that their teachers are either not communicating at all or are in fact plotting to overwhelm them, there is no reason why you cannot prove your students wrong and work to make their lives a little easier. The important thing is to evaluate how well your students are mastering the material, not how well they hold up under loads of work.

MISTAKE 79

Not allowing more than one day to complete homework…

When it comes to helping students not get overwhelmed with homework, another bit of advice I can offer you is to give students a few days to complete all assigned homework. In high school, my Geometry teacher regularly allowed us two days to complete any assignment. We were permitted to ask questions on the day between him assigning the work and us turning it in. There was never any excuse not to get work done in his class, and he was one of the most popular teachers in the school.

I am not saying you need to always allow multiple days for homework, but you might want to consider giving students a plan at the beginning of each week regarding what they will have to complete and turn in by Friday. If they understand early how much time they need to dedicate to completing your work, they can budget their time accordingly and schedule your assignments where they can most easily complete them. Allowing your students some flexibility does not diminish their effort, but it could improve their output.

MISTAKE 80

Assigning homework that is too hard for the students to do alone…

I strongly believe that homework, for the most part, should be something that a student can complete alone. While it is important that parents be there to answer questions and assist their kids with concepts and lessons they cannot understand, homework should not make the parent feel like they themselves are in school again.

For every complaint I read from a parent about their child having too much homework, there is a correlating complaint that **they** are spending hours of the night doing homework with their children. For some families, it seems that homework time has replaced family time! That should not be the case, and I cannot see how this helps children learn.

The homework you assign should not cover material you have not reviewed in class. Homework should be a review of the lesson you covered, not a preview of lessons to come. If students feel like they know — or are least familiar with — the material they are covering in their homework, they can both complete it faster and not feel frustrated while working on it.

I recommend that you remain flexible in your homework assignments. If you do not fully cover a lesson in class, tell the students they will have an extra day to complete their homework. Additionally, if the students do not seem to be grasping the lesson in class, cancel or extend the homework assignment until you have a chance to review it with them again. Remember, practicing something the wrong way serves no purpose.

Homework should be practice and reinforcement of something a student has learned — not a way to rope the parents into teaching something you have not completely covered in class. Remember that homework is for the student, not the parent. Assigning a student homework that they cannot complete on their own will only frustrate them, turn them off of the subject, and annoy the parent that they need to explain something to their child that you did not.

Often times, things that you teach in middle school and high school are things that parents do not remember, either. If it has been 20+ years since a parent has been in high school, it can be difficult to help a teen struggling with a physics problem or a complicated geometry formula. Keep in mind that you are the expert, not the parent.

Quick Review: When it comes to homework for middle school to high school-aged students, which of the following is TRUE:

A. You do NOT have to assign homework every night of the week.

B. You CAN give students more than one day to complete a homework assignment.

C. It is OK to cancel a homework assignment if you think your students are not ready for it.

D. All of the above

MISTAKE 81

Assigning tests or homework without paying attention to the school schedule…

By the time students reach high school — perhaps even as early as middle school — many are completely convinced that teachers actually pile on assignments and tests deliberately. Whether or not this is ever a temptation for you as a teacher, know that you can speak with other instructors and try to manage your students' homework and test schedules so they do not get overwhelmed. At the very least, space your work so that students have plenty of time to complete it.

If it can be avoided, do not assign tests at the same time as a major paper or project. Instead, space out your assignments so students have adequate study and preparation time for each project. It can also be helpful if you schedule certain tests or quizzes on certain days of the week so that students can rely on a certain level of predictability. That will help them learn to plan ahead.

Next, you should pay attention to holidays and school events when assigning work. For example, you might not want to schedule a test the day after the night of the school Christmas event. Finally, if you scheduled homework and/or tests on a day that turns out to be bad for the students, be willing to adjust your schedule. While you cannot be completely accommodating to everything that comes up throughout the school year, you should try to give your students their best chance for success.

Fair Testing

You will always have students who believe your tests are too hard or unfair. You cannot throw out test scores or accommodate every complaint. However, you can take steps to ensure you are conducting your testing in the fairest manner possible. Make sure your tests incorporate different ways of asking questions, and be willing to throw out a question if most of your students get the answer wrong. Consider the following mistakes you can avoid so that no one can falsely accuse you of being unfair in your testing.

MISTAKE 82
Only giving tests that leverage one way of learning…

As an extensive of the concept that "teaching for tests" is a bad idea, giving tests that only use multiple choice or true/false types of questions that fit well with standardized tests might fail to completely measure what your students have learned.

When I was creating tests for my classes, I tried to blend as many different types of questions in the tests as I could. Some students actually do better at short-answer questions or essays than true/false, where others do better with multiple choice answers than fill-in-the-blank. In order to provide all of your students with a chance to excel, it makes sense to leverage multiple styles of testing/question construction.

Furthermore, some students might not do well on tests at all but are good at making oral presentations or preparing poster boards on a special subject. You need to incorporate these types of opportunities when teaching and evaluating how well your students are mastering the material.

Remember that being creative and flexible in how you test, question, and grade a student will allow the majority of your class to express what they have learned, and it will give you a better understanding of what material your students have mastered.

MISTAKE 83

Not using a "curve"...

I am a big believer in giving a grade that the student earns. In other words, I do not advocate passing a student who has not reached decent subject mastery just so they do not have to deal with the shame of being held back. However, when I make a test, it is not a fool-proof process. When no student achieves an "A" on a test or very few students achieve a passing grade, there was clearly a failure in the preparation given to the students or the test itself.

No teacher should feel reluctant to provide some kind of "curve" on his or her tests. My fiancé's daughter had a teacher who graded the tests and then returned them to the students, allowing them to open their books, correct the answers they got wrong, and receive partial credit back for their corrected work. I think this is an effective way to assess what the student knows, and it allows him or her to learn from past mistakes.

Conversely, you can spend some time evaluating the test a bit and identify if there were questions that all (or most) of the students missed. In that case, you can review the question and see if you think it was badly worded or was something you did not cover sufficiently in class. If you identify any, throw those questions out, and re-grade the tests accordingly. Finally, you can just use a simple curve where the highest grade becomes an A or a 100 and adjust all grades from that point.

The important thing is that you realize that students talk to each other (and so do parents), and giving them tests where no one succeeds does not make you a "hard" teacher who demands a lot from students — it makes you look like a bad teacher who is not doing a good job. You do not need to "go easy" on your students so that you are well liked, but you do not want them to feel like an A is out of their reach or that success is unachievable, either.

I think this is an important matter for new teachers to understand, because, most likely, you have just come from a collegiate environment. Since the time I completed my master's in political science at the University of Florida, I have maintained a large network of college professors. We all know that teaching methods for college professors range from "relaxed and easy" to "sadistic." If you have had one — or more — of those professors that starts their class year off stating proudly that they have only given three A's in 20 years, your idea of grading and "curves" might have been skewed in the process.

Try to remember that these are children or teens, not adults, and success needs to be within their grasps. Do not be afraid to adjust your grading scale, use a curve, or provide extra credit to empower their success.

MISTAKE 84

Creating overly complex tests...

It is highly unlikely that many of your students will ever be able to understand the nuances of test questions that are looking for the "most correct" answer. Frankly, some of them might not be able to correctly answer any question that has more than one correct answer. Therefore, "all of the above" and "none of the above" answers might confuse them. That does not mean you cannot use those questions, just be aware that overly complex questions might fail to truly measure your students' understanding of the material.

When writing true/false questions, consider your students abilities as you decide how complex they will be. While the standard rule for true/false questions is that "if any part of the statement in false, then the entire statement is false," this is a concept that is more easily conquered by advanced students or certain kinds of analytical thinkers.

To help you decide if any question on your test is too complicated, look at how many of your students get the answer correct. If none or few of your students answered the question correctly, it might be that the question should be thrown out.

Finally, when preparing tests, if you know you have some difficult questions to include that will separate the A's from the B's, be sure not to put those questions at the beginning of the test. "If a student has major difficulty with the first question, it affects the rest of the test," says Bill Hayes.

MISTAKE 85

Not allowing enough time for students to complete a test...

You obviously cannot allow your students to spend hours on any one test, but do make sure you are not following some "minute per question" ratio that your students are not up to meeting. Be sure to spend ample time explaining the instructions for a test, and let the students know how long they will have to complete it. If it seems like very few students have turned the test in when it comes time to collect the tests, you might want to consider giving a little more time.

When you look over the test results, if it seems like the majority of your class was unable to finish or struggled with the end of the tests (in other words, they guessed), reevaluate how long you make your tests. While you cannot adjust your plans to suit every child in your classroom, you can make note of how most students are doing. If most students are doing poorly, you probably need to make things easier in some way.

Identifying & Dealing with Cheating

Cheating is probably not something you look forward to dealing with in your classroom, but you should definitely have a plan in mind for how to address the issue if or when it arises. If you think drawing a hard line on cheating will discourage the behavior in your classroom, you are probably correct. However, be sure that you correctly identify the student who is guilty of cheating, and hand out a punishment that is appropriate for the offense.

MISTAKE 86

Punishing the wrong student for cheating…

Perhaps you remember the story about my daughter — when my daughter was in third grade, she came home and told me she had her spelling test taken away from her because she might have been cheating. I received no note from the teacher, and I knew my daughter would have aced the test if she had been allowed to complete it, because I had reviewed the words with her all week.

I contacted the teacher and asked what happened. The teacher explained that my daughter and one of the other students were talking during the test, and she had to take the tests away from students who talked on the assumption of cheating. Thinking back, I cannot remember if this was the teacher's policy or the school's, because as she explained to me, this was being done in preparation for a state-wide standardized test that was being administered at that grade level.

The students had to practice their testing as if they were taking the big standardized test later that year, which would be strictly administered to prevent cheating. Since the results of these tests can impact the funding that schools receive and even a teacher's job security, I certainly understand why teachers and schools must prepare students on how to take such tests.

However, negatively impacting a good student's grades because someone speaks to them and they reply is not good policy. Fortunately, the teacher had enough flexibility to offer my daughter (and the other student) a make-up test. She easily made an A and learned a lesson about talking during tests.

My caution for new teachers would be to follow this example in one sense and learn from it in another. The only thing I think this teacher did wrong was not explaining to her students that she would permit the make-up test and not sending home a note explaining to the parent what happened and that there was a make-up option.

Otherwise, if you need to have a strict policy about talking during a test, permit a make-up option for students who are not cheating. Even if it is a harder version of the test, allowing students who engaged in a conversation that might have had nothing to do with the test itself to receive a grade is better than penalizing them with a zero. Furthermore, when one student talks, it could be to tell another child to keep their eyes on their own paper or to quiet someone who talked to them.

Assigning blame for cheating during a test or quiz is likely not a cut and dry issue, and an innocent student can easily get caught up in your discipline measures if you are not cautious. Be sure to listen to the students, and communicate with the parents. Permitting a "make-up" option for a first offense should not hinder your ability to keep up with your grading. If the problem persists with the same students, try rearranging the seating assignments. Also, remember that if you walk around the room while administering a test, you will automatically discourage a lot of cheating activity.

If the same problem occurs with the same students, schedule a meeting with the parents as the child might have some cheating issues that need to be addressed.

MISTAKE 87

Letting one student do everything on "group" assignments...

You need to be assigning group projects in middle school and high school for many reasons. Not only are you helping your students prepare for future college assignments, but you are teaching them valuable skills in the process. It is important to make sure to watch the groups and how they function to ensure that one or two students are not doing all the work while other students goof off and do nothing.

Some students are natural leaders or are so concerned about their grades that they want to take control of the work. These students will naturally enable more relaxed students to not put in their fair share of effort. In early grades, this dynamic might not be so bad. However, as students get older, one of the most common criticisms of advanced students is that they always ended up doing all the work on group projects.

The tendency for smarter students to willingly do all the work while other students goof off could have something to do with the tendency for gifted students to be introverts. According to recent studies, about 60 percent of gifted children are introverted compared with 30 percent of the general population. Furthermore, approximately 75 percent of highly gifted children are introverted (Silverman 2014).

While there are certainly advanced students who are extroverts, it is far more likely that you will find introverts among your gifted children. This means that while they are perfectly capable of carrying the load of a group assignment, they do not have the natural leadership and people management skills to make sure all members of their group contribute to the work.

Instead, gifted students will do the work of the group while resenting that other members are goofing off and having fun. After several years of doing this, these students will care enough about their grades in high school to just assume the role or leadership without even asking their classmates for ideas or contributions. This limits the learning experience for all students.

That is not to say that I think you should strike group work off your teaching methodology — though I am certain some introverts would be happy if I did. Instead, I am saying that you should carefully monitor your group work. Walk around the classroom, and sit in on the group as they discuss ideas and complete their assignment. When they all look at you wondering if you are going to give them instruction, tell them you are only there to observe and that they should proceed. Your quiet presence will ensure that for at least part of the time, all members of the group are paying attention.

As a college professor teaching nearly 50 students at a time, assigning "group" work and/or discussions might have seemed foolish, but I believed students could learn a lot from each other and that college is a place to see things from other world views. Therefore, when I assigned my students group work, I did just as I recommended above and sat in on each group.

Additionally, I asked them to "grade" each other's contributions to the group and factored those scores into their grades. Surprisingly, they tended to grade each other pretty well. I supposed they could have done this regardless of the amount of work each participant performed, but at least I provided them an outlet to express their opinion of their teammates work. I do not necessarily recommend doing this if the group members are best friends, but it is something that you can test out.

MISTAKE 88
Handling plagiarism...

Plagiarism becomes a more significant issue the older your students are and the more complex the writing assignments you assign become. It can take on a couple of different forms — your student can copy work word for word, your student can have someone else write the paper, or your student can simply forget to use proper citations in their paper. Each possibility comes with different issues to address, and the appropriate punishment varies.

First, if you are teaching older students and plan to assign research papers as part of your curriculum, you should have a plagiarism policy. Make sure you spend ample time teaching your children how to properly cite their references. If you find that your student has merely failed to use proper citations, you should grade them accordingly but not fail their total effort.

If you are teaching younger teens, and a student copies information word for word without using proper quotation or citing their reference, you should talk to them about plagiarism and citation, and give them an opportunity to correct their effort. While a student will not have this opportunity when they are older (or in college), it is reasonable to use this as a learning opportunity at this age.

The ability of high school and college students to purchase papers online is abundant. I know more than one person who earned extra money this way in college. However, this is considered cheating for both the person doing the writing and the person claiming the work as their own. If you believe your students have had a little too much help from a friend or their parents, talk to them about their effort. If during that conversation, you come to believe that the student needs to put more personal work into their paper, give them the chance to write it again with a small grade penalty.

Again, I realize that students have to become more and more accountable as they advance in age, but providing them the chance to complete honest work and still receive a grade (even if it comes with a penalty) will hopefully encourage them to do the work themselves in the future.

CHAPTER 11
Projects & Reports

Poster boards, book reports, presentations, and other projects are a great way to engage a student in learning and teach them several important skills. They are also bound to irritate the heck out of many parents and frustrate others to the edge of reason. Will you assign them? Of course, your more experienced co-workers who are parents themselves will as well. Will parents resent and perhaps even hate you for it? Probably.

While I realize that anyone can get into teaching at any point in their lives, if you are a recent, 22-ish graduate with your degree freshly framed, I understand that you may not yet be a parent. And if you are, your child is probably not in elementary school, let alone middle school or high school. Therefore, you have not had the delightful experience of helping your child complete one of the many creative learning projects you will assign.

My personal recommendation is that you borrow a niece or nephew, best friend's child, or neighborhood kid and give these assignments a "test drive" yourself before you roll them out to your classroom. If that is not a reasonable possibility and you still want to try to keep parents in your corner, pay heed to the recommendations in this chapter on things to avoid.

MISTAKE 89

Getting overly creative with book reports...

Teaching students a love of reading is possibly one of the most important things you can do as a teacher, and a love for reading can be instilled in a student at any point in their academic career. Of course, the sooner they learn to love reading, the better, but even a middle or high school student can have the world of literature open up to them for the first time under your tutelage. What could be a greater mark of your success than to be the teacher who turned your students "on" to reading? After all, if a person falls in love with reading, they will have whole world open to them for the rest of their lives. I certainly understand that beyond teaching students to love reading, you must also evaluate how well they are comprehending what they read.

A book report seems like an effective way to evaluate a student's progress in this regard. A book report's complexity should be based on the age of the student. You will expect less of younger teens than older ones, and you might think that making things a little "fun" will make the whole experience of giving a book report more enjoyable for your students. While you could be correct, be sure that you are not making things overly complicated for the parents.

Plenty of studies show the benefits of "engaged" parents, but now it seems like teachers operate as if they are assigning work to parents as well as the students. I fail to see why this is a valid teaching practice. As we've discussed previously, your student is the child in your classroom, not the parent. The parent has presumably already gone through middle school and high school and probably has a job, a house to take care of, and family to look after. In my opinion, any assignment given to a student should be something they can complete with minimal supervision from parents.

How do you know if the student could complete the assignment without parental involvement? Ask yourself if your students could do the project in your classroom while you monitor their work. If the answer is no, simplify the project. Of course, this recommendation applies to more than just book reports — it applies to any special assignment you give to your students.

On the specific issue of book reports, what you really need to do is make sure the students can communicate the important parts of the book such as title, author, key characters, significant plot points, and conclusion. Having your students create posters boards with pictures to illustrate some of those key elements could prove fun for your class, but anything more complex could just end up making the parents feel like they should have read the book in order to help their child complete the assignment.

MISTAKE 90
Assigning "art" projects for core subjects...

You are teaching your students about the Seven Wonders of the Ancient World, so what could be more fun for your students — and their parents — than an project to make a model of one of the "wonders" out of popsicle sticks and cotton balls! Do not expect much on Teacher Appreciation Day if you try something like this early in the year.

While there are many studies promoting the importance of art in the education of children, not all students enjoy it or are good at it. For them, an assignment like the one I just described would be pure torture. If you make it a "test" grade for a subject like history, then you just put what might be an otherwise really good history student at a serious disadvantage. When assessing how well students are learning a subject such as history or science, grading them for their artistic abilities is inappropriate.

In addition to an "art" project not being a good way to measure how well a student is mastering history or science, my recommendation about not assigning projects that children cannot complete on their own still stands. Making parents pull their hair out trying to come up with a design scheme for recreating the Hanging Gardens of Babylon out of foam is not the best way to endear yourself to them. Hand this type of assignment out right before winter or spring break, and you might actually get some angry letters.

Again, if you cannot picture supervising your students doing the assignment in your classroom, do not send it home for the parents to endure. Also, if you assign a project that requires more than a quick stop at a discount or thrift store, rethink the assignment. You should not send children home with a set of instructions that requires parents to stop by the hardware store. Keep things simple for yourself, the parents, and the students.

MISTAKE 91

Expecting parents will not be doing at least half the work…

If you do not heed either of the previous recommendations and proceed to assign your students a project that will undoubtedly require their parents to get involved, do not "grade down" if it appears parents have done "too much" of the work.

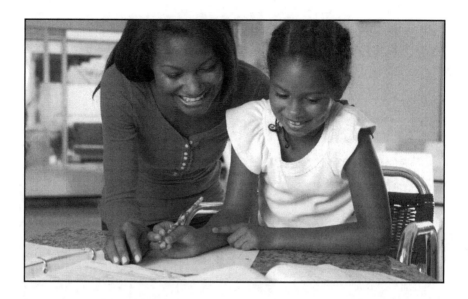

Once parents have to begrudgingly get involved in this type of school project, it is a bit unfair to penalize the student for needing that help. I admit that not all parents hate this type of thing. Some actually enjoy these artsy projects and cannot wait to sit around and help their children create the most beautiful replica of the Tower of London the seventh grade class at Washington Grover Middle School has ever seen. The other parents hate those moms and dads only slightly more than they hate teachers who give these assignments.

However, almost all parents understand that if they leave their children to their own devices, they will most likely fail to meet your requirements and will not do well on the project. Therefore, parents will get involved and will probably do at least half of the work, if not more. Most likely, you will be able to tell if certain students had help, but you will be unsure about others. It would be unfair to take points off some projects without knowing for certain that the other students did not have help.

As a result, these projects should probably involve research and should be graded solely on the basis of whether or not the students followed the instructions.

MISTAKE 92

Assigning science projects that are just reports...

Once a child reaches middle school or high school, a science project should take on a certain meaning. It should involve a hypothesis that can be tested, measurable results, and a conclusion. Therefore, a science project is not a report about bees.

While a history teacher might expect students to create poster boards about a subject that you want them to research, parents expect science projects to be more complicated. If you decide to assign a science poster, try to make it something that the student can research and assemble relatively easily. Otherwise, the parents of your students will learn a great deal about bees, but the students may retain very little. Furthermore, if you have the students do some of the research in your school library, you can make sure they are learning how to do research while putting less pressure on the parents.

CHAPTER 12
Student Nightmares

Almost everyone has something — perhaps more than one something — from their school years that they were forced to do that they absolutely hated. For some students, it might have been bad enough to elicit small panic attacks. As a teacher, you should know that there are some things you will need to "force" your students to do and other things you can give them a break on.

While public speaking is a skill that students need to form a basic, rudimentary ability in, not every child is going to grow up to give mass speeches on a daily basis. As a result, a student might need to deliver a short presentation in front of the class at one point or another, but you do not need to repeatedly call on a quiet child in an effort to involve him or her.

There are many ways to assess if a child is mastering the material you are teaching. And ultimately, you are not grading a child on how well they talk in front of the class or how well they do board work — you are only evaluating whether or not they can perform the skills you have taught. If you sense that an exercise causes a child stress, try to minimize how often you ask him or her to do it.

MISTAKE 93

Calling on students at random to answer questions…

You might think this is a good way to gauge who is paying attention and to measure how well your less outgoing students are grasping the material. The problem is that a child might be failing to raise his hand not because he is daydreaming or is unaware of the answer, but because he is uncomfortable speaking in front of the class. I am not suggesting that you only call on students who volunteer 100 percent of the time, but perhaps you do not need to catch a student completely off guard to accomplish your goal.

Try telling the students ahead of time that you will be asking questions of each student in order, starting on one side of the room at the start of the row and continuing back and across until each person has had a chance to participate. Make it clear to the students that if they do not know the answer, all they have to do is say so and that there is no reason to be embarrassed.

When you use a strategy like this, the student knows a question is coming and what it will likely pertain to. They can also prepare themselves ahead of time to tell you if they do not know the answer so that they do not have to fear your disapproval if that is the case. The student also knows everyone else in the room will be answering questions as well, so at most, they will only be called upon once, and then they can relax.

MISTAKE 94

Forcing children to do board work...

Brandy Mayer, a self-proclaimed introvert who works as a Clerk of Courts in New Orleans, told me that as a child, she hated things that put pressure on her in school. Being forced to do problems on the board was a particularly high negative. "It freaked me out and made me dread classes," she said.

I am not a natural introvert, but I was shy as a child. Yet, I never minded working a problem on the board and it never really occurred to me that some people feared such exercises. But that is the thing about children, and especially teens — you cannot tell what will fill them with fear and what they can easily brush off. Keep this in mind as you engage with your students, and if you can tell that one is particularly uncomfortable with an exercise, let them skip it if you can. If you are required to assess students in that manner, minimize the amount of times you have to ask them to do it.

Remember that children are not likely to tell you bluntly what makes them nervous or uncomfortable, so it is up to you to pay attention.

MISTAKE 95

Making children share something about themselves…

A teacher asking students to tell everyone their name and share something about themselves is about a common of a practice as using a No. 2 pencil on a test. However, it is a practice that many people — even adults — positively hate. By the time students reach high school, they have probably started rehearsing this little introduction, but even so, they may have no idea what to say.

This practice in school actually translates into what is commonly referred to as the "elevator speech" by the time a person is of the right age to participate in a career search. Therefore, I cannot deny that it is a good practice to start preparing students on how to make these little speeches. However, you may want to provide them guidance.

Rather than asking teens to tell the class something about themselves and leaving it as a general, open-ended direction, go ahead and give them specific guidance on what information to share. Ask them to talk about their families, favorite color, hobbies, or summer activities. Simply helping students narrow down their choices can reduce their anxiety over answering this question. In the worst scenarios, be sure to make it clear that their name is sufficient.

CHAPTER 13
Subject-Specific Guidelines

There are a host of errors you can make when teaching any one specific subject, but this chapter focuses on a few common ones along with explanations as to why you should avoid them. These are not hard and fast rules, and certainly not all teachers will follow these recommendations, but you might find that if you avoid these tactics, your students will perform remarkably better.

MISTAKE 96

Not requiring students to show their work on math tests…

The idea of showing work infuriates some people. They insist that it is not necessary, and to a certain point, the might be true. However, as math becomes more complex, having students show their work will help you evaluate what they are doing wrong when they answer incorrectly. Without work shown, it is almost impossible to pinpoint what the child fails to understand. They might resent showing work at first, but if doing so helps you help them to improve their grade, it is worth the annoyance.

MISTAKE 97
Making students read out loud to the class…

There are a host of reasons why having students read their books out loud to the class is probably not the best use of your time. Among them is the fact that many of your students will disengage and only pay attention to what is going on when it is their turn to read. Other students will simply believe you are wasting their time with a mundane or even lazy approach to teaching. However, some will dread this approach for an entirely different reason — they hate, or even fear, reading out loud.

If you want to have students read to the class, limit the length of the passage, and then open the floor up for discussion afterward. Have a different student read a short segment and ask students for their thoughts again. This type of back and forth dialogue will help students cover material in their book while keeping them engaged in a discussion of meaning. If no one seems too nervous during these activities, you can try longer segments.

On the other hand, if this seems to work for your class but you want to evaluate an individual student's reading abilities better, try to have them read in small groups, pairs, or to you individually as a classroom exercise. This might take longer to evaluate, but you will probably get a better sense of their capabilities, because fear will not negatively impact skill.

MISTAKE 98

Overemphasizing date memorization in history...

There are many dates in history that are significant, but try to make history lessons about something more than just calendars. Spend significant periods of time on key events and talk about the people involved in the events you are studying. When you ask a question on an exam, combine other key information with the date to trigger the student's memory. For example, instead of just asking "What year did Christopher Columbus discover the New World?" Ask something like, "In 1492, what famous explorer sailed from Europe and discovered the New World?"

MISTAKE 99

Not teaching students proper safety measures in science...

Science is an area where as students get older, knowing and following proper safety measures are very important. If you are having your children work with microscopes or Bunsen burners or any other such science equipment, make sure they know all the rules for use and storage.

MISTAKE 100

Not testing students on spelling rules…

Do not just teach children to memorize their spelling words each week and forget them the next. Teach them and test them on the rules of spelling. If they can understand the rules of spelling, they will become better long-term spellers than if they just remember how a single word is spelled. English is extremely complicated in its spelling rules, and there are exceptions for every rule you learn. This is a complicated area to teach, and you should probably not grade too harshly, but do try to incorporate it into your spelling grade.

MISTAKE 101

Not working with students on their handwriting…

Many, many schools across the country no longer require students to learn cursive writing. The general thought process regarding handwriting is that ultimately children will do more typing than anything else in their academic careers. While this may be true, it is still incredibly important that a student's handwriting be legible. You and other teachers need to be able to read their work on tests and homework among other things. If a student's writing is bad enough, they could get marked wrong for material they actually got correct. Do not let a student pass your grade without working to improve illegible handwriting.

CHAPTER 14
Grading

Assuming you are not one of those teachers who takes great pleasure in being impossible to pass or one who feels like they must give certain amounts of C's and D's to be taken seriously, you will likely want to help your students bring their grades up. Let me first say that I do not believe in handing A's out like the professors at Harvard apparently do (where recent studies show rampant grade inflation and an average grade per class of A-) (Stein, 2013; Strauss, 2013).

However, I do believe that any teacher can strive for their students to get as many A's and B's as possible without fudging their test scores to accomplish it and without considering themselves a failure for not having students who do more poorly. With that being said, helping struggling students bring up their grades should be a large focus of any teacher. This section is dedicated to advising first-year teachers on how to do that in an effective and efficient manner.

MISTAKE 102

Not grading participation...

Having taught several college courses, I have structured my grading scale in numerous ways. I find that I do not like grading attendance, but I do believe it is important in regards to grade participation. There are numerous ways to do this when teaching adults, but I believe it is a mistake not to find some way to apply this concept to middle and high school students as well.

While some students are shy, which makes it difficult to draw them out of their shells, many are open, full of questions, and are more than happy to "participate" in learning activities. Engaging a student in participation activities is a great way to keep their little minds from wandering, to prevent them from getting bored, and to really help them grasp a lesson.

Since participation is a valid way to learn, you should put some grading emphasis on it. If you plan to make 10 percent of your grade a participation grade,l and setup activities to evaluate that grade, you are encouraging yourself not to skimp on this aspect of learning.

Additionally, a student who engages in class by creating and presenting a topic on a poster, talking about a book they are reading, or acting out a skit on a segment of history he or she is learning demonstrates some subject mastery. Even if they are not able to translate that understanding of the subject into a perfect test score, they should receive some credit for their work. A minor participation grade not only helps students engage in class, but it can also bolster the confidence of a student who might not test well but is still learning.

MISTAKE 103
Grading for neatness...

My junior year of high school, my literature teacher demanded that we submit rough drafts for our papers. He jokingly — I think — told us to find the "Pigpens" of our school and let them hold our papers for a couple of hours so that our rough drafts would be appropriately messy and in need of improvement. His joke serves to remind us that some teens are just plain messy. While their parents are likely still living in blind hope they will grow out of this stage, you have to decide how much emphasis you are going to place on neatness when it comes to grading.

In middle and high school, it is likely that children have developed a certain level of small motor skills. If they are deficient in this area, they will probably always be lacking in this skill set. Ergo, you may not want to make neatness too much a part of your grading scale. Also, when thinking of projects and posters as mentioned in previous sections, try to remember that not all students enjoy — or are even good at — coloring or drawing. As a result, coloring or drawing something they know they will be graded on might cause them a great amount of anxiety.

Therefore, when you assign a coloring or drawing exercise, be sure to let the students know they should do the best they can at being neat, but you will be grading for factual accurateness or for "correctness." In this manner, your non-artists will not become worried about having their grades hurt when they otherwise know the material but just cannot color or draw well.

MISTAKE 104

Not grading for neatness...

Conversely, there are times when students need to learn to achieve a certain amount of neatness. If you cannot read their handwriting at all or they write their numbers and letters without paying attention to the lines on their paper, you might need to take some points off in order to get them to try harder in this area.

The simple fact is that if students cannot learn to write coherently, they will be marked wrong on tests and homework assignments where they may actually be correct. If you can help them achieve a level of neatness in their writing that is legible, this will benefit them in all of their future academic pursuits. While you do not need to be punitive in your grading for students who cannot draw, you might need to consider taking off points for students who are extremely amiss in their writing abilities — particularly if you are confident that if they took their time, they could do a better job.

When to award or take off points for neatness might very well end up being a judgment call on your part, but you should probably work into your grading system some kind of policy you can communicate to your students and apply it evenly across the board.

MISTAKE 105

Not giving extra credit...

I am a big believer in extra credit. I feel if a student is on the cusp of a higher grade and they want to put in some extra work to bring it up, they should be given the opportunity to do so. I think extra credit is a good practice to begin even with elementary-aged students.

Personally, I would advise that you plan it into your tests and curriculum. Provide bonus questions on tests and assign extra credit sheets for every nine weeks. However, if you do not plan on giving extra credit but your students ask about it, be quick to accommodate it.

It does not take a lot of extra work to give your students an extra credit assignment, even if you plan it at the last minute. The extra grading might be a little inconvenient as nine weeks or the semester winds down, but not all of your students will do extra credit, so the additional work for you will not be that significant.

I have heard teachers say that "only the good students" do extra credit work or "only the students who do not need it do the extra credit." These teachers believe that the practice is a waste of their time. Having taught hundreds of adults, I can assure you that the extra credit I have given has made a difference for many of my students.

It is important to teach children that even if they do not master the material completely early on, a little extra work can make a difference. Additionally, I think working on extra credit helps student realize that a teacher does care about their grades and is willing to put in a little extra effort to help them improve.

As many of you first-year teachers can probably recall, being able to talk to your professors in college makes a difference in academic performance. Rewarding children for asking for help or extra work is a good way to develop the confidence to approach teachers that will one day immensely benefit their educational pursuits.

MISTAKE 106
Not giving all of your students the chance to do extra credit…

Of course, once you decide to allow your students the opportunity to do extra credit, you need to extend that offer to all of your students, not just those who ask for it and not just those who need it. While you might be able to identify the students it will help and those it will not make a difference for, to avoid any accusations of favoritism or unfairness, offer extra credit opportunities to your whole class.

MISTAKE 107
Not offering before or after school help…

I know teachers put in long days, and, as a first-year teacher, you need to avoid getting overwhelmed and burned out. Perhaps the thought of offering before or after school help sessions just does not appeal to you at all. Maybe you think you need that time to take care of other matters so it is possible for you to go home and not have a mile-high pile of things to do at home.

I am not suggesting that you offer these little help sessions every day; I am merely suggesting that once or twice a week, you should offer students the

Chapter 14: Grading

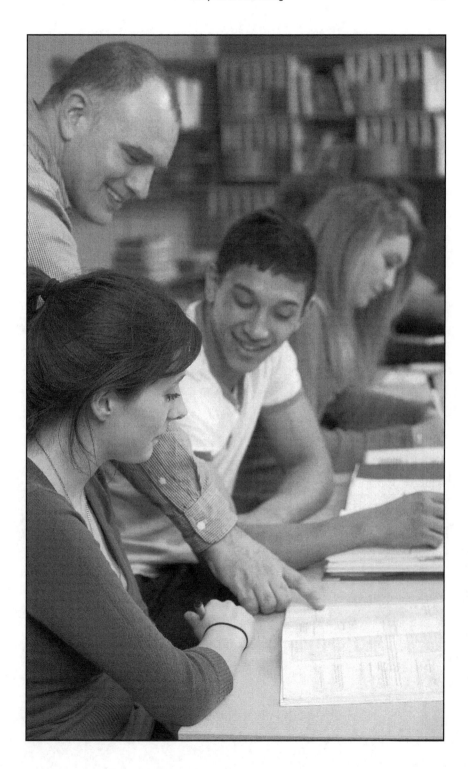

opportunity to meet with you to go over work they are struggling with in the class. Your school might offer free tutoring for students, but that is likely to be generic tutoring designed for passing standardized tests. The help sessions you could offer would be more in line with the lessons you are teaching and would be more beneficial to your students.

In order to avoid getting too stressed out or burdened by before and after-school help sessions, you can structure that help time to cover certain subjects on specific days and ask students to sign up for the help sessions so that you know how many children to expect. I have also seen teachers adopt a policy that they will only offer help sessions to students with grades of C or below. This will help ensure that your time is spent with students who need your help the most.

Offering help sessions like this before and after school and making sure parents are aware of this option can also go a long way to defusing any animosity toward you if a child ends up not doing well in class. I highly recommend finding a schedule that works for you and adding this into your weekly routine early on in the first nine weeks.

MISTAKE 108

Not leveraging what the student is good in to help them with their weak areas...

I believe that you can help a student improve by using what they excel in to help increase their understanding and performance in areas where they are weak. For example, if you have students who enjoy artwork, use their creative and visual talent to draw pictures of the lessons you are teaching. If you have students who are talented writers, readers, or storytellers, try to tie those skills into their math lessons.

The reason for this recommendation is simple — everyone is good at something and using that "something" to help make other subjects make more sense can prove to be an excellent teaching tool. Do not be afraid to use a wide-range of teaching methods to communicate your subject matter, and if something is not working, do not be afraid to change your strategy to something that works better for your classroom.

Try to remember that you designed your class material for students you did not know — for nameless, faceless students whose strengths and weaknesses you were blissfully unaware of. Now you know these children, and you know what their interests are and what they do well, so now you can customize your existing lesson plans around these individuals you have the privilege to teach. Be flexible, and use strength to promote more strength.

MISTAKE 109

Not calling the parents soon enough...

In a separate section of this book, I discuss how important the parent partnership is for you in your teaching efforts. This is as true when it comes to academics as when it comes to classroom discipline. Open and frequent communications with parents will allow them to keep their children on track and correct academic slips before they become too severe.

I recommend that, on top of progress reports at the mid-way point in a nine-week grading period (which most teachers provide), that you should also make sure parents are aware of their child's grades on a weekly basis. I have seen teachers achieve them by sending home test packets for parents to sign or a weekly communications log for parents to initial. Using any idea to keep an open dialogue (even through notes) between you and parents is a good idea.

Leveraging this weekly, open dialogue between you and parents will help you make them aware of a poor grade or a series of poor grades so they can take action before a progress report or report card is issued. Most parents will be grateful for such opportunities because they will want to correct their child's issues or decline before it becomes more serious or too late to address.

In addition to these forms of communications, if you are really concerned about a child's academics, I would recommend that you set up a conference sooner than later. Again, the earlier the parent is aware of negative academic performance, the sooner he or she can help correct it, whether that is making sure the child attends your help sessions, getting the child external tutoring, or helping the child directly.

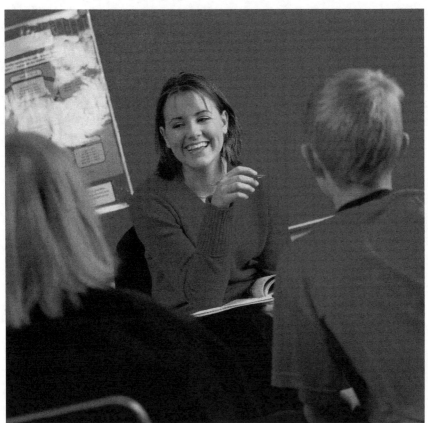

MISTAKE 110

Not giving the student the grade he or she earned...

No matter how hard students try, sometimes their grades will not reflect their effort. And yet, "A for Effort" should not be part of your thinking. If you have done your job throughout the school year, working to identify tests you need to curve, assignments you might need to drop since no one did well on them, providing opportunities for extra credit, and so on, then you have to give your students the grades they earned.

When you are looking at the final grades, there is no telling what exactly is going to bother you. It may be a student that you know tried really hard, but still ended up with a C. It could be a child that is otherwise a straight-A student, but makes a C in math. It could be a student that you have to fail in a subject area because no matter how hard you both worked at it this year, the student just could not grasp the material at grade level. Do not be tempted to "pad" grades if you feel bad. You need to be able to justify those grades and show that you are being fair across the board. Whatever rules you apply to one student, you must apply to all.

MISTAKE 111

Being unwilling to fail a student...

In a previous section, I discussed in length the mistake of not using a "curve" when testing. However, there is a difference between curving a grade on a test or tests and padding students' grades to pass them when they would otherwise fail.

Our education system is rampant with the idea that failure will hurt a child, injure their self-confidence, and apparently cause insurmountable damage to their success. The pressure is so strong to pass children that many students get promoted without learning the necessary skills they need to advance. This ultimately leads to a portion of the population graduating while functionally illiterate, or even worse, students who are allowed to walk on graduation day but are not receiving diplomas — just certificates of attendance.

In the attempt to not ever make a child feel like a failure, you can often fail to give them what they need, which is an education. Your students should not be taught that failure is the worst thing that can happen to them. Instead, they should be taught that not learning from their failure is the worst thing that can happen.

As a teacher, advancing a student who is not prepared is a mistake. Now, I am not talking about a student who is excelling in all subject areas except for one. That student should be able to catch up and keep up with the demands of the next grade level adequately enough. I am talking about a student who has not mastered enough of the material to pass your class.

The plain simple truth is sometimes you have to fail a student, give an F, or hold a child back. It can turn out to be the best thing to happen to the child. They get another year to learn and understand the material, and when they do advance, they can confidently face their next school year. A failing student can become a good one with another year of practice under his or her belt.

Conversely, passing a student when he or she is not prepared to face the next school year can do more to erode his or her self-confidence. While your student might get to stay in the same class as all of his or her friends, that student will continue to struggle, make bad grades, and feel inadequate to the tasks that are put before him or her.

While I am certain that as a first-year teacher, the last thing you want to do is fail a student. You might even wonder if that student's failure is your fault. Do not let your insecurity prevent you from doing the right thing. If you have offered help and extra credit and worked one-on-one with the student, then you should be able to judge if they are ready for the following school year. If you feel they are not, then do them the favor of holding them back.

MISTAKE 112
Not keeping track of grades well…

One of your most important jobs as a teacher is to evaluate your student's performance and document the results. The subsequent results must be recorded accurately and completely in order to make up the student's final grades. Your school might have a method of recording grades they expect you to use, but you still need to be sure you are organized and methodical in your approach. You do not want to send home graded papers with students before you record them in your grade log. Keeping track of your grades effectively will help you greatly if any student — or more likely, parent — challenges your grades at the end of the year. Failing to have a good system could leave you in a lurch.

MISTAKE 113

Emphasizing that grades are everything…

It is extremely important to let your students know that grades are not everything. One of the sharpest professors I ever had in college told us that she never worried about her grades — she simply did everything as well as she could and focused on taking in all the information rather focusing on the grades she got. It is no surprise that she walked out of college with a nearly perfect GPA.

When your students start to focus on the letter grade assigned to their work, they will start tailoring their output in order to get that grade. You want to make sure that you are creating a great learning environment, and in order to do that, you have to emphasize the importance of learning in order to be educated, not in order to see an A on the report card.

PART THREE

WHAT YOU TEACH & HOW YOU TEACH IT

You studied for years to earn your teaching degree and probably even worked to be certified in specific subject areas. You know your material well and are excited about teaching it to your students. However, you may or may not be happy with the state-approved curriculum you have to teach, and you may soon learn to despise standardized testing and all the implications that come from the results. If only teaching was as simple as educating students on history, science, math, or language.

But it isn't, and there are many mistakes you can make when teaching your material, and an even greater number of errors you can make when testing or evaluating your students on what they have learned. This section is dedicated to reviewing things you should avoid in regards to teaching, homework, testing, grading, and the like.

CHAPTER 15
Classroom Dictator or Mr./Ms. Softie? Does being liked matter?

For the majority of the individuals reading this book, one thing might be true: you want your students to like you. You probably even want them to love you. Go ahead and admit that and get it out of the way. This book covers 199 mistakes new teachers make and how to avoid them, but wanting to be liked too much is probably at the top of most "do not" lists for teachers everywhere.

Wanting to be liked could cause you to be too lax in terms of discipline. It could also lead you to use too many "fun" activities in class and not communicate the lesson. While you might not want to think of them this way, young children can sense weakness in their supposed leaders. If your students believe they can manipulate you or guilt you because of your desire to be well-liked, this could cause you to lose control of your classroom without even realizing it.

Of course, you do not need to come to the conclusion that the inverse is true — that if wanting to be well liked is a weakness, not caring what your students think must be a strength. No. If you come across as completely unfeeling or uncaring, you will not be able to create a bond with the students, which could make it more difficult for you to engage them in learning. You should not strive to be hated, just like you should not let the children walk all over you just so you will be loved. Read on to learn how to avoid mistakes at either extreme.

MISTAKE 114
Wanting to be everyone's favorite teacher...

If you were inspired to become a teacher because of your favorite teacher(s) or because some movie inspired you to teach and make a difference in the lives of your students, being loved by your students probably matters to you a great deal. Even if you have other motives for teaching, you still probably want to be liked by your students — after all, that does make teaching easier and more productive. Besides, who would turn down being named "teacher of the year?"

The most important thing for you to remember as a new teacher is that being loved or liked cannot be your No. 1 objective. You need to earn your student's respect and admiration, and being liked — or even loved — will naturally follow. Plan your classroom activities to foster an atmosphere of learning and success rather than "fun," and you will make a lasting impact on the students. You see, it is not the teacher that was entertaining that sticks with you as much as the teacher who finally helped you master multiplication or made sure you could read as well as the rest of your class. Ultimately, you will be remembered for what you taught your students, not how "cool" you were.

MISTAKE 115

Responding emotionally to a personal attack...

During all the preparation you have done to get ready for your first teaching job, it may have never occurred to you that a student might insult you. If a student gets upset, angry, hurt, or frustrated, then they might say something mean or hurtful to you. Recognizing that this is a possibility and preparing for it ahead of time could help you keep your cool and maintain a professional demeanor in the face of a painful verbal attack.

If you were teaching young children, the "mean" thing they say could be as simple as "you are not my mommy" or just an emphatic, loud "no, you can't make me" when you are giving them an instruction. But you are teaching teens, and they might not be so kind in their back talk. You could encounter insults such as "you are fat" or "you are ugly" and other things that might cause you discomfort on a bad hair day. Even worse, you could hear far more vulgar versions of the above from students who are better at insulting you than you could have ever imagined.

First off, recognize that you are dealing with teens — even if they look like adults — and they do not have a solid measure of beauty, health, or appearance. Resist the urge to wonder if the five pounds you have gained is starting to show or obsess about a blemish you saw in the mirror that morning. The same child that called you ugly one day might say that you are the prettiest teacher in the world the next.

My second piece of advice is not to take insults personally. It is far more likely that their insults to you are a reflection of their inability to do their work or frustration over understanding a concept than a testament to what they think about you. While teens might be good talkers, they are not necessarily good communicators. They lack the ability to distinguish what is upsetting them and address it. Instead, some will lash out and try to hurt someone else to distract from their feelings of inadequacy. Sadly, some adults do not grow out of this habit.

Even if you do take their comments personally, do not show it. Responding emotionally to a student would damage your image of being in control of your classroom and could cause other students to lose respect for you. The best things you can do are maintaining your self-control and addressing the student's outburst in accordance with your discipline policy for your classroom. If that means sending the child to the principal's office, do so in a calm and controlled manner.

Once you have addressed the outburst from the student, feel free to give your class an assignment that will allow you to regain your composure on the inside if you need to. Halt your lecture and give a reading assignment so you can sit at your desk for a moment and calm down internally. The biggest thing you need to achieve is to not let your students know you were shaken. Do not get angry and yell; do not get hurt and cry.

MISTAKE 116

Not staying professional when a student is crying…

While both of my children were perfectly fine with me dropping them off their first day of kindergarten and displayed not an ounce of fear or concern, I realize that some children are not so exuberant about this change of life. To encounter crying in a kindergarten class is not unheard of and is probably to be expected.

However, crying does not suddenly stop when kindergarten is over — teens might even be more likely to rush out of your class in a heap of tears for a variety of reasons. Consider the following:

<u>Crying over grades</u>: When my daughter was younger, she occasionally cried when she did not make a perfect score on a test. I can only imagine how this mystified her teachers considering she did well, just not perfect. Of course, other students might cry when they fail a test or do badly on an assignment. In any of these cases, you will want to offer them comforting words without minimizing the importance of studying and testing well or doing anything to change the grade they earned.

<u>Crying because they are different</u>: As I have mentioned in other areas of this book, teens are keenly aware of what makes them stand out from their classmates. Depending on their personalities, they might like their uniqueness or hate it with a passion. You may find that even without being picked on, a student can feel so uncomfortable about their differences that it can produce tears. If a student admits this is the reason why they are crying, be kind and help them calm down and participate in class again. Do not ever tell them they are crying for a stupid reason, no matter how tempting that might be.

<u>Crying because of rejection</u>: Bullying, teasing, and harassment are certainly things that could make a child cry, and they must be addressed by you in order to foster a positive atmosphere for learning. However, sometimes your students might not be engaged in these bad behaviors at all, and a child will still feel rejected for one reason or another. If a child feels unpopular, unaccepted, or disliked by the girl or boy that they have a crush on, tears can follow. You must speak to these issues quietly and gently so you can minimize the amount of distraction this causes your classroom.

<u>Crying because of home life.</u> Any number of situations could fall into this category, from the first grader that misses his mommy to the 14-year-old who just learned her parents are getting a divorce. If a student opens up to you about her home life, comfort her the best you can, and decide if this is a situation that you can handle in the classroom or if she needs to see the guidance counselor. Just remember that while you should be considerate of tough times that students face at home, it is still your job to teach them. You can allow these students some extra consideration, but do not pad their grade or forgive poor performance. Not teaching them will not make their home life better, and it will do them a greater disservice in the long run. Consult your guidance counselor if you need help figuring out the best way to handle a child going through a tough time at home, and remember to balance the needs of that student with the need to keep your entire class on track academically.

MISTAKE 117

Letting a classroom get out of hand while having fun…

Every now and then, you want to let your students engage in learning activities that are unique and even fun. Just be cautious not to overdo these activities or let them get out of hand. Of course, you want learning to be fun for your students, but you also need to make sure they are still in fact learning. Additionally, you need to tailor your lessons for the age-range you are teaching and the number of students you have in your classroom. An activity that works well with 10 students might get out of hand with 25.

MISTAKE 118

Being unwilling to explain yourself…

While you are certainly the king or queen of your classroom, and your word is law so to speak, being unwilling to explain yourself to your students — at least a little — will do you little good in terms of earning and keeping their respect.

You are there to teach, and students are there to learn. If you adopt a complete philosophy of "because I said so," you could be failing to instruct your students. That is not to suggest that you need to explain ad nauseam every classroom policy or decision you make. I am only suggesting that when a student asks "why," it is occasionally OK to explain your reasoning to them.

Furthermore, if a child is asking questions about a subject, there might be a misunderstanding in place between you and your students. If a child has failed to understand a lesson or an assignment from you, letting that continue could damage the learning process. This is not a question of whether or not you are liked; it is a question of whether or not you are understood.

Do not adopt an attitude of refusing to repeat or explain yourself at all. While you do not want to let your students lead you off course in the middle of a lecture, ensuring that they understand the word or examples you are using is pivotal to communicating your message.

It is understandable that you might not want to allow students to ask questions while you are in the middle of a lecture. Allowing too many questions is a sure way to get derailed and permanently off-topic. If you adopt such a policy, be sure to have a dedicated question and answer time before you cover too much material. Also, evaluate how well your students are engaged at several points during a lecture. If you look out on a sea of confused faces, it might be time to back up and make sure your students are grasping your meaning.

MISTAKE 119

Not admitting if you are wrong…

Let us say you had the flu, did not get any sleep, was nearly hit by a very poor driver on the way to school, and broke a nail five minutes before your lecture. All in all, you have a litany of excuses as to why you suffered the horrible indignity of actually being wrong in front of your class. Still, do not operate as if it did not happen. Correct the error and move on. You are not here to teach your students inaccuracies and misinformation.

MISTAKE 120

Being too relaxed...

A portion of this book will address mistakes you can make when disciplining a child, but it is important to remember that another discipline mistake can be having none at all. There is a phrase saying that many first-year teachers do not understand until it is too late: "Do not let them see you smile until Christmas."

You are probably wondering why in the world you would want to come across so harsh early on, but the idea is simple — start tough, because it is far easier to relax than it is to regain control if you have lost it.

Have a plan for discipline that complies with your school standards and is well communicated to your students. Be prepared to reiterate several times at the beginning of the school year and

follow through with it early so that students believe that you mean what you say. Remember that making ideal threats will not help you build respect. You might think you are being merciful or helping them learn the new system, but you are teaching them that they can get away with breaking your rules to an extent. Instead, make sure you back up your words with deeds.

CHAPTER 16
Relating to Students that are Different from You

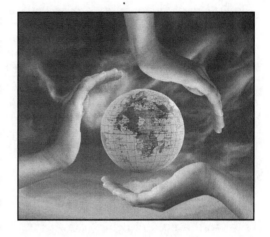

While they say that "opposites attract" when it comes to romantic interests, the truth is that in almost every aspect of your life, you will find it easier to relate to those with whom you have shared interests or similarities than people with whom you cannot find common ground. Shared history, something as small as being born on the same day, or finding that you love the same movie can form the basis of a future friendship.

It is not surprising that you will find it easiest to relate to teens with whom you share common ground. The students who are different than you are the ones you may find the most difficult to manage — not because they are poorly behaved or are not teachable, but simply because you have more of a gap to bridge. This chapter is dedicated to helping you identify areas where you might need to work a little harder to ensure you are properly reaching your students.

MISTAKE 121

Continuing the extrovert vs. introvert "war"...

According to Jill D. Burruss and Lisa Kaenzig's article "Introversion: The Often Forgotten Factor Impacting the Gifted," most teachers report being extroverts. This is not very surprising since the school experience — particularly the elementary school experience — is designed to favor extroverts. From an introvert's perspective, the day is full of large common areas and large classes, even bigger groups for lunch and physical fitness, and little to no opportunities to be alone and decompress.

By the time a student reaches high school, they may have enough flexibility to find their down time. They can choose to sit alone at lunch and read for a bit, they can elect to take a study hall in the library, and they can avoid some experiences that would make them the most uncomfortable. A middle school child does not have that much choice in how to structure their day, so be patient with them.

One thing you need to remember is that an introverted child is not just "shy" and in need of being "drawn out of their shell." You do not need to help them make friends with everyone else in the classroom; you only need to help them find their niche. By niche, I mean that even introverted children need to learn certain social skills, and they definitely need to be able to participate in class activities.

However, whenever possible, you should incorporate teaching methods that make the introverted student more comfortable into your teaching strategies. If you can, allow the introverted teen some alone time while other students work in groups. I am not suggesting you purposefully alienate any child, but if you give your students the option of grouping up or working alone, you can watch them decide for themselves what makes them more comfortable. This is a process you should observe closely and remember for later.

Some suggestions for introverted students include independent study, small group instruction, collaborative learning activities, tiered instruction, role-playing, journaling, quiet time, and book clubs (Burruss 1999). Remaining aware of the fact that children can be introverts and that these children might end up being some of your best students will help you prepare yourself to teach all personalities. If you can be the teacher who helped the introverted child operate at their best rather than trying to help them "be like all the other students," you will make a lasting, positive impression.

MISTAKE 122

Not being able to communicate with different personalities…

While it can be simple to explain people as either introverts or extroverts, the truth is that personality types are very wide-ranging. There are so many more elements to what makes someone tick than whether they are reserved or outgoing. In order to effectively teach your students, you need to be able to understand their personality types and adjust your communication style accordingly.

For example, you may come across a student that is always a distraction — perhaps they interrupt you during class or it seems that their main goal is to get you off-topic. It may be that this student craves attention for one reason or another (maybe they do not get enough attention at home), so they turn to disrupting your class to get attention from his or her peers.

This is just one example of a varying personality type that requires you to look deeper than surface-level. Do not just assume that a student is acting a certain way because they are trying to be annoying — many times it can be a quirk of their personality, or it is a deeper issue coming out in a strange but understandable way.

MISTAKE 123
Trying to impose your political beliefs on your students…

Children are sponges, ready to absorb information and opinions and perhaps even adopt them as their own. In fact, political scientists looking to predict election outcomes have polled elementary-aged children on who they would elect president and found the correlation to actual results uncanny. The Scholastics News election poll has correctly called 15 of the past 17 presidential elections (Quercia 2012). The simple conclusion is that children accurately reflect the political opinions of their parents, including thoughts about hot-button issues such as abortion, gay marriage, support for war, and immigration.

Even though you are teaching older students, it is still unlikely the child has enough life experience to properly form an opinion about these matters. Therefore, whatever comes out of the teen's mouth, they are probably getting from their parents. Should the student say something you strongly disagree with, try not to state your opinion in the classroom. If you want to keep parents on your side, the last thing you need to do is have Jim or Sue go home and tell them you said they were wrong about hot-button issue x, y, or z.

If the students in your classroom express varying or opposing opinions, you can open the classroom up to discussion of the subject, but be sure to encourage polite debate, not flat out arguing. And be sure to never tell your class who you think is "right" or "wrong."

The one exception to this rule is that you should correct opinions that carry a hint of racism or prejudice in order to make sure all of your students feel comfortable in your classroom. While it is sometimes obvious when a child is a member of a minority, it is not always the case. You should remind your class that it is important to respect other people's religious beliefs, political affiliations, or culture. This could cause some conflict with parents, but you need to stand firm and explain to them that you have students in your classroom from different cultures, and it is very important that you create a learning atmosphere free of bullying. Even if they do not like your stance, they will likely support it.

CHAPTER 17
Recognizing Outside Influence on School Work

While it would be nice if every classroom were an island to itself so outside influences could not distract from your teaching or your students' learning, that is not reality. Some outside influences are internal to the student (such as learning disabilities), while others are external factors (such as a sick sibling or parents divorcing).

It is not your job to solve all of your student's problems, and no matter how much you might want to, you probably will not be able to be their hero if things are going poorly at home. However, you can recognize if these outside influences are affecting a teen's work and try to help the student overcome whatever issues or challenges they are facing.

MISTAKE 124
Assuming a student has a learning disability if they do not…

While you should pay attention to a student's behavior and look for signs that they have a learning disability, you should not quickly assume you know what the problem is and allow this conclusion to shape your opinion of your student. Instead, you should make notes about the student and their performance. If you have well-structured concerns, bring these issues to the attention of the parents and perhaps your campus nurse or counselor (particularly if he or she is a trained psychologist).

You might feel that you see the child often enough to be able to correctly assess what medical problems they face, but you simply do not know enough about the child's background and medical history to pronounce a child ADHD, bi-polar, or autistic. You should leave such diagnosis in the hands of medical professionals who will include you in the process, but only as one voice in drawing their conclusions.

If a parent opposes medication or is resistant to the idea that his or her child has a learning disability, it is important that you do not overstate how strongly you disagree with him or her. Again, let the child's pediatrician walk him or her through this process to determine the best course of action. That way, your relationship with the child's parents is not damaged in any way, and you can more effectively work together to ensure the student can overcome and deal with any learning disability they face.

Additionally, if you are incorrect, and there is no learning disability, you might damage your relationship with the parent for no reason. For these reasons, present your observations to the parents without passing judgment.

MISTAKE 125

Not tailoring work for a child with a physical or learning disability…

Should a child be diagnosed with a learning disability, tailoring their work to accommodate these concerns is vital to your success as a teacher and theirs as a student. Once you have been made aware that a student has a learning disability — whether at the beginning of the school year or later — you need to make any necessary changes that such a disability requires.

Depending on the learning disability the child has been diagnosed with, there could be no change on your part, the child could need to spend time with special teachers, or you might just have to administer some tests verbally instead of in written format. How much you need to adjust to accommodate a student's needs is different in each circumstance, but there is no question you will need plan.

One of my friends in high school had moderate to severe dyslexia. We routinely looked over her work to edit her spelling and grammar and helped her in math. These subject areas can be very difficult for a child with such a learning disability, but that does not mean the student does not grasp the material. Be sure that you know your school's requirements for testing and appraising students with learning disabilities, and comply with them. If for some reason your school has no defined rules or policies, work with your students to provide oral exams and other ways to properly evaluate your students' understanding of the material.

In addition to teens with learning disabilities, you might also have a student with a physical disability of some type. Schools have significantly more resources for people with physical handicaps than they did when I was young, but that does not mean that you are off the hook for having a teen with a disability in your classroom. It is important that you learn how to work with such students to help them achieve their full academic potential.

In order to determine the best course of action for the student, you might need to consult with their parents, other teachers, and school resources, such as counselors. Follow the advice of your colleagues, and make sure you follow any laws or regulations that might be applicable in these instances.

MISTAKE 126

Dealing with a physical or learning disability inappropriately...

While I am sure that you covered topics like this while earning your degree, I believe it is important to emphasize that a learning disability does not mean that someone is stupid. Unless you are a special education teacher, you probably will not be teaching students with severe emotional and intellectual impairments. If a teen is in your classroom with a learning disability or a physical handicap, it is one that can be overcome in the course of normal academics. Even with a severe learning or physical disability, a student still might be incredibly intelligent.

Hopefully, in this day and age, you would not let someone's gender or nationality form preconceived ideas in your head about what he or she may or may not achieve. In the same vein, do not let a diagnosis of a learning disability or an obvious physical handicap lead you to conclude that a student is not highly intelligent or does not have a strong capacity or appetite for learning.

Chapter 17: Recognizing Outside Influence on School Work

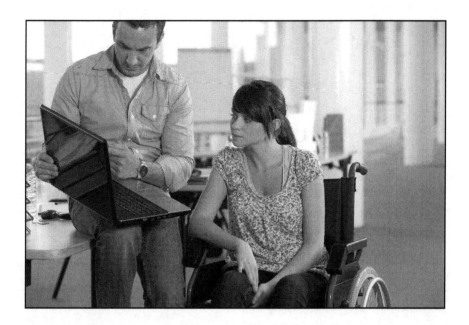

Keeping an open mind to learn and discover a student's capabilities beyond a learning disability or physical handicap will be an essential part of you being a good teacher to those students. If you conclude early that there is something they cannot do or some material they cannot master, you may have falsely limited these children. While you might have to tailor your methods of teaching or testing for the teen's individual needs, do not conclude that the student simply cannot learn.

As mentioned above, make sure you work with the parents, experienced colleagues, and school resources (such as the nurse or counselor) to identify a teaching plan that will promote success. Learning disabilities or physical handicaps do not equal a lack of intelligence, and you might find yourself surprised by what your students can achieve if you challenge them to excel.

MISTAKE 127

Ignoring a sudden drop in grades…

I do not expect that even as you record grades throughout the course of your first year, that you will always know where your students stand in all subjects academically. However, between nine-week grading, progress reports, and just general testing, I do believe you would be capable of noticing if a student suddenly drops in academic performance.

If they only drop off in one subject, and you are tackling new material at that time, then the slip might easily be explained. However, if you notice an all around decline from a student, you might want to consider talking to them about what is going on in their lives, at home, or otherwise that is causing them to have a hard time with their school work.

There are numerous issues that the student could be facing to cause a decline in grades, and some of them are actually rather easy to address. At times, children might be facing a difficult home life or even something more serious like molestation. Other times, it could be that the child's eyesight is starting to fail and they need glasses. Whether the problem is complex or simple, making note of a sudden drop in grades and addressing it will do your student a world of good.

I recommend that you begin by talking to the student. Hopefully, Sue or Jim will quickly confess if questioned that they are having a hard time seeing the board or that the words on the page are starting to look fuzzy. Some students fear anything that will make them look different, and the idea that they will need glasses might cause them enough distress that it will take you talking to them and making their parents aware of the situation to get the problem addressed.

Once you rule out concerns like failing eyesight or hearing, you can start to talk to the student about their relationships in the classroom. If the child is being picked on or teased, that can cause a distraction from their work. Something that might signal this problem is if their homework is perfect, but they're testing poorly and doing badly in class. Again, a student should be willing to talk about being bullied if you create a safe atmosphere for them to talk — not with other students present. Feel free to enlist the help of your school counselor as you meet with the student if you think this is the issue.

If you feel like through talking with the student and your general observations of the classroom that the problem the child is facing is not social with their peers, it might be time to ask them about home life. Again, you might want to ask a more experience teacher or your school counselor to sit in on such a meeting. What a child reveals to you could range from their sibling being sick to parents fighting to problems with sexual or physical abuse.

In such cases, you will need to take action, but you will also want to make sure you take the correct action. If you have involved a colleague, they should also be able to help you figure what to do next. Your school counselor and principal should help you determine if law enforcement or other state agencies need to be involved.

The idea of a child confessing to you a serious problem or abuse issue might make you fearful, but it is important that you do not shy away from such challenges as you teach. Your main job might be to educate your students, but you are also there to be their champion and maybe even their hero. Whether you were the first person to recognize they need glasses or the person who gets them the help they need to no longer be abused, you can be the difference in their lives.

So pay attention and do not overlook signs — like falling grades — that something is amiss and needs to be looked at more closely. You will regret it later if you do.

Teens with difficult personal lives

As noted in earlier chapters, teens can face any number of difficulties growing up. There are many stressors and bad things that can happen to children that should never occur, but denial does not make these things go away. An adolescent can face abusive parents, emotional struggles as parents separate and divorce, or just sadness if a parent or sibling is sick.

While you were learning all you thought you needed to know to teach, you might not have been instructed in what to say to a teen whose parent is in the military and deployed overseas. You might not have been told what to do if a student's brother is diagnosed with leukemia and all the parent's focus turns to the sick child. No matter how much you know it happens, you might not know what to do for children who are being abused. This section does not have all the answers, but it provides you with stories and advice from teachers who have faced these challenges and lived to tell the tale.

MISTAKE 128

Favoring one parent over the other during a divorce…

Divorce is hard on teens. There is not a way of making it easy on them — even in the most amicable of splits. If one of the parents has been active in supporting the classroom or has been the one to always show up at parent/teacher conferences, you might find yourself drawn to support that parent. Or you might have some other bias based on school gossip about why the parents are splitting. You cannot show that to a student or to the parents. Not only is it unprofessional, but it does not benefit the student in any way.

No matter what a student says during a divorce or which parent he or she gets mad at, most likely he or she still loves both parents a great deal. He or she does not want to hear bad things about his or her mother or father or hear about how one parent is better than the other. They might want to know whose fault it is, but that is only because they want to know how to fix it. What you need to do is reassure your student that his parents love him, and that will not change.

If a student is having a difficult time in your classroom, and you know this is going on at home, schedule a time for them to talk to your school psychologist. Also, bring the parents in for a conference, and talk to them about how they can provide their child the consistency he or she needs to keep doing well in school. While parents sometimes end up using their children to hurt their former partner, most parents only want what is best for the kids even in the middle of the divorce. You cannot fix their marriage, but you can support them as they try to make things easy on their children.

MISTAKE 129

Not being flexible if the student has stress at home…

You need to be consistent in how you handle the classroom and not show favoritism, but to show zero flexibility when a student is facing a difficult time at home does not advance learning. If a child was sick, you would allow him or her time to make up work. If a child's sibling or parent has a disease, or the child is concerned about a parent stationed overseas, this can be far more distracting than getting over the common cold.

In order to reconcile how you work with a student facing a difficult time with the need to be consistent, adopt a general policy of how to handle these situations. Do not allow a student to use a bad situation to not do work or to use your pity to raise his or her grade, but do have an idea of how much time you will allow to complete a missed assignment or if you can help them through extra credit. Have a policy that you would offer any student in a difficult situation — after all, odds are good that not all of your students will be facing a difficult home life simultaneously.

Once you determine how much extra flexibility or time you can afford, consult your colleagues and school resources to see what help might be available for before or after school. Whether the student needs tutoring or extra time with the school counselor, getting other people involved will help him or her get what he or she needs while taking some of the burden off of you to make sure he or she can still succeed academically. You do not have to go through this alone. Getting support will be beneficial to everyone involved.

MISTAKE 130

Basing a student's grades on things they have no control over...

If you are teaching a subject like band where attending a performance is a requirement, it is perfectly reasonable to factor that into your student's grades. However, be sure not to base too much of your student's grades on events that occur outside of the classroom.

Even if your students are 16 or older, you cannot expect them all to be drivers and in command of their own schedules. Furthermore, they also cannot control events such as traffic, car breakdowns, illnesses, and any number of other reasons why they might end up missing a performance. If a teen explains to you that they were unable to attend a mandatory event because of their parents, you should probably allow some flexibility in your grading.

As such, while it is important to teach children the value of following through on commitments, be sure to allow your students to be excused for missing mandatory events if their parents offer you a legitimate reason for their absence.

MISTAKE 131

Promising silence if a student confides in you...

The things a student could tell you in secret range from the heartbreaking (the little sister has cancer) to the infuriating (someone is touching them where they should not), and it can be challenging to deal with. It might be hard to break a promise or to violate their trust when they confide in you, but sometimes, that is exactly what you must do. If you are unsure how to do it, seek help from a coworker or school therapist.

There are protocols you can take to intervene in the proper way, and those steps should be followed. If the end result of you revealing the information a student shares with you is going to be a prosecution, then you need to work with the police to make sure they are able to build a strong case against the wrongdoer.

No matter how anonymous you might want to remain, even if you have to break your word, someday, they will understand.

When the situation is just one that is sad rather than something that needs official interference, you might be free to keep the secret. However, if you start to feel uncomfortable or get the impression that the parents should be made aware of their child's feelings, talk to the school counselor on if/how you might approach them, or try to talk your student into approaching her parents herself.

Chapter 17: Recognizing Outside Influence on School Work

MISTAKE 132
Not seeking help from the school counselor…

If you have a trained psychologist on staff, it seems like a waste not to consult him on any issue you are not sure how to deal with in regards to your students. Your school's guidance counselors are not just an asset to you because of their experience, but also because of their training. There is little reason for you to try to figure out every situation by yourself.

While not all guidance counselors will have experienced every challenge a teen could endure, they likely have more first-hand experience and training in this area than you do at this point in your career. Seek their help not just to protect your professional hide, but also because helping children through difficult periods of time is why they work for the school.

CHAPTER 18
Relating to Parents/ Guardians

If you thought being a teacher only meant working with students, then you have missed half the equation. Parents are your partners in education and should provide you with all the support you need to maximize your teaching efforts for their children. While that might not always be the case, you should still give parents every opportunity to engage with you and be an active component in their child's academics.

Furthermore, the relationship you form with the parents of your students can have a great impact on both the student's performance and the impression your principal forms on your work. If you develop a negative relationship with some of the parents, that can cast a dark shadow on your classroom and lead to several complaints finding their way to your boss. While you do not want to walk on eggshells in fear of what parents might say about you, you do need to keep in mind the downside of bad people skills in your profession. In order to maximize the likelihood that parents will end up singing your praises to the principal at the end of the year, avoid the mistakes described below.

Communicating with parents regarding grades and student progress

You might think that if you are having no behavioral issues in your classroom than there is no reason to contact parents. You would be wrong. While parents might consider "no news – good news," when it comes to bad behavior, many appreciate proactive communications when it comes to grades. Parents do not want to be blindsided at the end of the year with your impression that a child should be held back. Nor do they want to only hear about a child not doing their homework after they see a "D" on a report card.

Whether or not a parent is highly communicative with you, most assume that you will make them aware of issues they need to act on. If you notice that a child is late to school frequently, missing classes too often without notes from the parent, or other behavior that could lead to the child failing, go ahead and call the parents.

MISTAKE 133

Not communicating with parents in writing…

If you are having trouble with a student, be sure to communicate with the parent — in writing — what your issues are and the potential punishment the child faces. If you can send e-mails, save your side of the communication, and request an e-mail receipt. If you can only leave them messages or send notes, keep dated copies of your communication to show your efforts to reach out to the parents.

While it is not pleasant to think of a parent filing a complaint against you, some adults are more likely to blame the teacher than to hold their children accountable for behavioral issues. The more you can do to prove you tried to reach out to the parents, the less they will be able to argue against you at a later date.

MISTAKE 134
Not sending work/tests home regularly...

As I mentioned before, many parents are actually excited to see the results of their children's work. Additionally, you really do not need a backlog of student work taking up space on your desk. Make every effort to regularly grade, record, and send home test and assignments.

MISTAKE 135
Letting parents call the shots...

While it is important to be constantly in touch with your students' parents, you need to make sure that you are keeping your authority. You are, after all, the teacher here — you went to school, you got your degree, and you are now an expert in your field. Do not let a conversation with a parent dictate how you run your classroom. Make sure that your conversations with parents are structured and informative, but do not let the parent take over and change the way you run things. In most cases, the parent is not trying to be critical of you — they just want the best for their child. Be open to suggestions, but remember to be firm and trust in your own expertise.

MISTAKE 136

Not reporting behavioral issues…

Even if you are just having minor behavioral issues with a student in the classroom, you should still send a note home to their parents. It is very frustrating from a parent's point-of-view to deal with an escalated situation when you heard nothing about the little steps that led to the "crisis" along the way. Be sure to communicate with parents when you are having issues; you might find those problems are easily corrected just by letting the parent know what is going on at school.

MISTAKE 137

Not scheduling parent-teacher conferences…

It is very important to schedule parent-teacher conferences on a semi-regular schedule. You may want to do it when it is time to send home progress reports or report cards. You might want to schedule conferences just with the parents who have concerns. No matter what your strategy is, be sure to leave yourself open whenever a parent might want to meet with you.

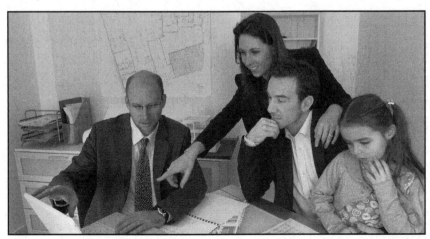

MISTAKE 138

Waiting too long to tell parents you think there is a learning problem...

Part of building a solid relationship with parents means establishing an open line of communications early and keeping it flowing throughout the school year. When a student is excelling and demonstrating excellent behavior, it is easy to talk to parents. However, you might feel intimidated when the student starts to slip in behavior or grades. You might have even heard horror stories of parents blaming the teacher for their child's bad performance and feel that any communication might spell confrontation.

The first thing you need to do is relax. Talking to and working with parents can be more beneficial than you can imagine. In the majority of cases, no one knows a child's strengths or weaknesses better than his or her parents. They might be able to provide you with insight that can help you improve the child's performance, and you can provide them with guidance on what they can do at home to help their child succeed.

The mistake of not communicating with parents early on only gets worse if the child's performance continues to slide. I have a good friend who still speaks ill of one of his daughter's kindergarten teachers years later, because that teacher never mentioned a problem with the child's learning or academic progress until the end of the year when she called him in to discuss holding the child back. He insists that progress reports and report cards never indicated his daughter was struggling, and he had no idea that the teacher felt his daughter was lagging behind until it was nearly too late to do anything about it.

Of course, I cannot speak about the teacher's point-of-view in this instance, but assuming this parent is telling the tale close to the truth, there was a serious break-down of communications between teacher and parent in this case. Additionally, that parent might have a real complaint to bring to that teacher's supervisor. If you are in your first year of teaching, you definitely do not want to get caught in this situation.

Remember that your first priority should be helping the child achieve academic success. Even if the parent proves unresponsive, your attempts at communication will prove that you have done all you can to advance the success of all of your students. Even if you do this for no other reason than to protect yourself, I believe you will find it immensely beneficial in the long run.

MISTAKE 139
Blaming parents for not supporting a student at home…

The last thing you want to do with parents is to be confrontational, even if you are upset with them for the lack of support they show their child at home. When you sit down with a parent that you feel is not providing your student the right amount of support, do not lecture them on what they are failing to do for the child.

First, that is likely to create an adversarial exchange where they blame you for their child failing instead of listening to what you have to say. Second, it really will not help solve the problem. You need to explain in what areas the student needs to improve, how they can help that student to improve, and what the student needs to do better.

Communicating with the parents openly may or may not change the support that your student receives at his or her home, but blaming the parent for your student's failures will not help the situation, either. In order to keep positive relations going between you and the parents, keep things cordial. Try not to be overly judgmental on their parenting, and perhaps they will not be unfairly judgmental on your teaching.

MISTAKE 140
Blaming the parents if a student is badly behaved at school…

There are numerous online posts and websites extolling the idea that if the child is bad, the parents are doing something wrong. While it might be the case that your most ill-behaved or spoiled child is the product of over-indulgent parenting, it will do you little good to approach parents for help with a child's behavior while playing the "blame" game.

On occasion, we have to put the responsibility of a student's behavior squarely on the student's shoulders. The older the student is, the more likely the possibility that bad behavior is coming from the student's own desires, choices, or motivations. A student can be motivated by the desire to "be cool" or to impress a girl/boy. They can also be acting "tough" because they are afraid of getting picked on.

If a student is a disruption in your class, the best approach is to try to work with the parents to correct the situation. Should you come to believe that the parent is part of the problem, you will have to work around that situation. Still, avoid being resentful toward a parent even if they do not act as your immediate ally. Things can change, and cultivating a positive relationship with the parents might prove beneficial to you — or a fellow teacher — down the road.

MISTAKE 141

Not clearly communicating what the student can do to improve...

In addition to not blaming a parent for a student's poor grades, you must also accept that the responsibility of communicating what the student needs to work on and how they can improve his or her grades is really on you.

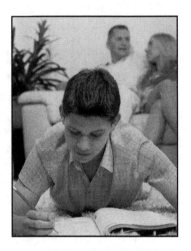

There are many intelligent, dedicated parents out there who will look over a child's grades and tests and work to identify what their child is doing poorly in. If they can properly identify what their child does not understand, then these parents might even be willing and able to work with their child to correct their poor performance. **These parents are not the norm.**

Most parents will expect that you alone are their child's teacher, and it is your job to teach them. The average "engaged" parent will probably make sure their child gets their homework completed and may even go over their homework with him or her to make sure they got everything correct. That same parent might even review some study material with their children before a test, but parents have their limits. These limits often come out during science projects, so tread lightly there.

If parents start to feel like they are doing more work with their child than you, then they might become bitter and resentful. *"I should just homeschool my child for all the work I do them with after school,"* or, *"Exactly who is teaching my child — me or their teacher"* are shared sentiments among many parents I know. You really do not want to contribute more to the idea that teachers are not doing their jobs during your first year of teaching.

When you communicate with the parents of your students in regards to grades (be it on progress reports or at parent/teacher meetings), be sure to explain to the parents what their child can do to improve. Furthermore, if one of your students is performing particularly poorly in a subject or two, be sure to communicate information to the parents regarding after-school help or tutoring.

If you approach parents in this manner and provide them with tools to help their children improve, then you will create a feeling of teamwork and collaboration between you and the parents. That sense of cooperation is the best thing you can do to help your students thrive, and it will prevent a host of complaints about you later if you have to counsel parents to hold back their child.

MISTAKE 142

Not telling the parents if you think the student might have a learning disability…

You are new to your job, and this might even be the first time you have worked with a large group of students on your own. You probably do not have a psychology degree, and you probably are not a medical doctor. So if you observe behavior in a student that might be considered indicative of a learning disability, do you speak up about it? Would the parents listen to your opinion? If other teachers have not noticed this and have not talked to the parents by now, are you even sure you are right about this?

These questions and doubts are all perfectly reasonable in your first — or even first several — years of teaching. It is one thing when a teacher with 20 years of experience who has worked with hundreds of students tells a parent, *"I think you should have Tommy tested for dyslexia."* It is quite another when a 20-something-year-old tells a parent that his or her child might have ADHD. Right?

Perhaps the older, more experienced teacher does have a better foundation to form their opinion, and perhaps the parents will not listen to you. You could even be wrong. Sharing your concerns and thoughts about a child's behavior or challenges in your classroom with the parents is never a bad idea. If anything, talking to the parents could be the beginning of a discussion they need to have with their doctors and other professionals, or it could be the last note of confirmation they need to tell them what they have already suspected.

While it would serve you well to consult other teachers in the school and/or the school guidance counselor and nurse, it is in the end up to you to sit down with the parents and tell them your concerns. You do not need to present your opinion as fact to these parents — after all, you lack the expertise and years of experience to be sure of anything. Opening up the lines of communications with the parents is not a mistake, and you might learn something from the parents that explains the behavior you have noted.

MISTAKE 143

Letting your personal opinion of a parent show...

It takes all kinds of people to make the world go around. You will have parents you think poorly of for many reasons. You will see mothers who dress like prostitutes, and you will have fathers you think look completely unkempt. You will also see fathers or mothers with new wives or husbands that seem far too old or too young to have a kid.

There will be parents who do not answer your calls or emails. There will be parents who are argumentative or rude to you. On the other hand, there will be parents who are influential in your town or obviously wealthy. There will be parents who drive fancy cars or wear expensive jewelry. There might even be parents who could do you personal favors.

For good or bad, do not allow your opinions show to your students. Treat all of the parents with the same professional regard and respect. Not only do you need to make sure the parents do not pick up on any favor or disdain you have for them, but more importantly, you need to make sure the students do not figure out who you like or dislike.

Young children will probably think their parents are amazing. But the older they get, the more they will become aware of the social norms of their community. They will be able to look around and see if one parent dresses differently (better or worse) than the rest. Children will be able to figure out rather easily whose parents are impressive and whose are not. What you want to do is maintain an aura of being neither impressed nor put-off to your students.

Teens cannot help if they are born into a poor family or a well-off one. They have no control over how their parent dresses or speaks. They do not deserve to be looked down upon or disrespected solely because of their parents. If you send cues to your students that you have an overly strong positive or negative opinion of their parents, you might inadvertently make the child believe that that opinion carries over to them.

You want to make sure that your children believe the classroom is a place of equality — a place where if they work hard, they can receive the grade they deserve. You do not want to create the illusion that some children are favored or held back because of their parents. Treating all parents the same will help your students realize that you are judging them for them — not their parents.

How to deal with divorced parents

Dealing with parents is difficult enough, but dealing with parents who do not like each other or work together is even harder. Unfortunately, with the marriage success rate in the U.S. being about 50/50, the chances that you will have students with divorced parents or even parents going through a divorce during the school year are likely. You must figure out how to navigate this land mine with grace and a strong focus on what is best for your student.

While the parents will be dealing with loads of negative feelings, they will not always be keeping their focus on what is in the best interest of their children. Even the best meaning parents will have lapses and failures in this regard (and, of course, not all parents have the best of intentions). In order to avoid having parents dislike and be uncooperative with you, read on for some basic strategies on dealing with divorced parents.

MISTAKE 144

Communicating with one parent, but not the other...

In most divorce situations, friends and family will be forced to "choose sides." You are the one exception to that rule. Not only is there no need for you to favor one parent over the other, but it is also ill-advised for you to do so.

You will encounter both the parents who are already divorced and those who are going through one. No matter how custody is split between the parents, unless one parent has a court order disallowing the other information regarding their child, it is best that you keep the lines of communications open with both the mother and father.

That does not mean you need to send two sets of paperwork home so the child can take it to both sets of parents. But if you send email notifications to your parents, be sure to include both parents on those lists. Make sure you schedule parent teacher conferences with both the mother and the father if you need to communicate with them regarding grades or behavioral issues. Try to make sure they both know about school events, such as plays and holiday events.

Parents have a lot of work to do in a divorce setting to make sure the child does not need to choose between her mother or her father. How parents decide to split up school functions is really up to them. You just need to do your job and make sure information is communicated to both parties, and let them figure out the rest.

MISTAKE 145

Appearing to favor one parent over the other...

If you know a parent because they are highly involved with their child's schooling (say they have brought in cupcakes on a birthday and chaperoned a field trip), you might be tempted to favor them if a divorce occurs. Or you might see bad behavior during the divorce and come to favor the other parent as a result. Worse yet, you might have really been friends with the couple before you taught their child, and you have a natural loyalty to one of the two parents.

None of this matters when it comes to professionalism and how you should conduct yourself as their child's teacher. Communicating with both parents is still important, being considerate of both parents is still important, and engaging both parents in a positive way when you see them is still important. Do not allow the drama of divorce to enter into your classroom.

Furthermore, while your student might be very upset with one of his parents, he still love them very much. Your teen does not want to think that one parent is the "bad guy," and if you appear to take sides in this conflict, you could damage your relationship with your student without even realizing it. Even if you do not negatively impact your relationship with the student, you will almost certainly destroy it with the parent you badmouthed. To do your job well, you need a positive working relationship with both parents, especially during a divorce. Always keep that in mind.

MISTAKE 146

Being unwilling to communicate with a step-parent…

While I have advised you to be Switzerland when it comes to divorced parents, and I can certainly understand you not wanting to get involved with parent and step-parent bickering, you still need to proceed with caution when it comes to keeping a step-parent out of the loop.

When you talk to a student, you might find that it is their step-parent who does his or her homework with the child or the step-parent who helps him or her study for tests. If this is the case, not speaking to a step-parent because an offended mother or father does not like you doing so will hurt your student. Think of it this way: if the schooling parent hired a tutor, would you refuse to talk to that tutor just because the other parent did not like it? If the answer is *"of course not,"* then think of the step-parent in the same light.

If you are concerned about issues of confidentiality or privacy, consult with your school's principal. Most likely, all you need to know is what the custody arrangement is and if one legal guardian has consented for you to consult the step-parent. Again, if other legal issues are present, your principal can help you work it out.

In the worst-case scenario, you might be unable to talk to the step-parent, because the school does not want to risk getting sued or dragged into the court battle. You should not be unwilling to work with step-parents when it benefits your student and you are able to do so.

Teaching Family

If you find yourself teaching in the town you grew up in (which is quite common), the chances are good at some point that you will teach a family member. The family member could be as close as your own child or niece/nephew or more distant like a cousin's children. When this occurs, your first instinct should be to request that the school reassign the student. If that cannot be accommodated, you should take precautions not to be perceived as unfair or bias.

MISTAKE 147

Not making administration aware of the relationship...

Of course, the first mistake you can make is not making administration aware of the relationship between you and the child. They can hardly try to rearrange the classrooms if they do not know there is a potential area of conflict.

MISTAKE 148

Letting the child call you by a name the other students cannot use...

If you do end up having to teach a family member, let them know that while they might call you "Aunt Trish" at home, in the classroom, they need to address you as "Mrs. Robinson." You are not doing this as an attempt to hide your relationship with the child from your other students, but just trying to leave the impression that all children in your classroom are on even footing.

MISTAKE 149

Working too hard not to show favoritism...

While you need to make every effort not to show favoritism to a family member, do not go too far in the other direction and become unnecessarily harsh toward or ignore the child to whom you are related. Parents who coach their own children tend to vacillate back and forth between wanting to make their kid the "star" unfairly and being harder on their child than anyone else on the team. Your goal is to treat your family member the same as your other students, not better or worse.

CHAPTER 19
Relating to Other Teachers

One of the most valuable assets available to a new teacher is other, more experienced teachers. Chances are good that no matter what shocking or challenging situation arises during your first year of teaching, one of your colleagues has experienced the same issue and will have some advice to help you handle it. Therefore, it stands to reason that forming and maintaining good relations with your fellow teachers is an important part of your professional development. This chapter will offer guidance on mistakes to avoid in your efforts to create solid working relationships at your school.

MISTAKE 150
Not asking for guidance if you need it...

If you are reading this book, then you are clearly interested in avoiding mistakes. Your first year of teaching — well, any year of teaching, really — can be full of challenges and can be overwhelming. Many first-year teachers get burnt out and are just plain exhausted long before they get to summer vacation. If you get tired or frustrated, your students will suffer. Do not be afraid to ask for advice and use it (and sick days — you get to use those when you need them).

One of the biggest mistakes inexperienced teachers — well, professionals of any kind, really — make is wanting to cover up their inexperience so much that they do not ask for help from their colleagues or supervisors. You coworkers and supervisors can help you, and in many cases, they have quick, easy advice to give you that can make your life easier. Ask questions, seek guidance, and leverage your associates' ideas so you can be better at what you do.

MISTAKE 151

Getting involved in campus politics…

Schools have their own versions of "office politics," and getting involved in them can prove detrimental to any teacher, but especially so to the "new guys on the block." Just as your students might have squabbles, grudges, and backstabbing, so might your coworkers. The best action you can do is to steer clear and stay quiet.

If there are instances where you have a "vote" in a matter, listen carefully to what others have to say about the individuals up for a position and participate in the election, but do so without drawing attention to yourself.

Chapter 19: Relating to Other Teachers

MISTAKE 152

Getting caught up in gossip...

Like any work environment, gossip will circulate a school. People will discuss each other's personal lives, professional behavior, and at times cross lines that should not be crossed. While technically talking about anyone behind his or her back can constitute as gossip, there is definitely positive and negative talk. Discussing how you love someone's idea for a fundraiser is vastly different than speculating why someone's husband never comes to school events.

While it might seem like listening to campus gossip is an easy way to start to fit in and bond with your co-workers, it could prove detrimental to your working relationships or even your career. Even if gossip seems harmless, it can lead to you getting caught up in the campus politics mentioned in the previous entry and make you someone that another teacher now has a grudge against.

Also, as you will recognize with your own students, your reputation will be shaped by the company you keep, so just listening to someone else gossip can hurt you. Find a way to politely excuse yourself from conversations when this sort of activity comes up. Do not be concerned about what people will say behind your back when you leave the room. Just conduct yourself as you should, and soon, you will earn the respect of your colleagues.

As an addendum to this mistake, do not gossip with other teachers about students or parents. OK, yes, students talk about you, and parents do as well. And yes, by the time I graduated high school,

I realized that teachers talk about students and parents, too. It takes place in just about every teaching lounge across the country. However, it is still best to avoid as it can cause problems; if you are new, it is far more likely to hurt your career than to help it.

MISTAKE 153
Passing along a false allegation…

One of the worst side effects that can come from gossiping is passing along a false allegation. Whether the allegation comes from a student, parent, or another teacher if it is something that should be brought to a principal or supervisor, do it, and then wait and see what happens.

Reputations can be damaged in an instant and can take an eternity to repair. Even being vindicated from a false allegation cannot always repair a damaged reputation. While there are some things that cannot be ignored, it is best that you do not help convict someone of something before all the facts are known. If a teacher is accused of misconduct, abuse, sexual harassment, and other inappropriate behavior, your best course of action is to make the necessary report and let management take action. Just understand that accusations are not always true, and spreading gossip will not benefit you if turns out to be a false report.

If, after watching management's course of action, you decide the situation was handled badly, you might need to make some decisions on going over your supervisor's head or going to the school board. That is a worst-case scenario that you will hopefully never face, especially not in your first year of teaching. Even in that case, gossip will not help you. You might need to seek advice, but do so one-on-one with someone you respect and trust.

CHAPTER 20
Teaching in a Politically-Correct World

On the flip side of the same coin of favoritism is showing disdain for any one student or group of students. The first thing you should probably ask yourself is if you do have any preconceived ideas about people based on race, gender, religion, etc. I am not asking you to call yourself any of those "ist" words that you want to avoid being labeled as by parents or administrators. I'm suggesting you ask yourself if you are prepared to teach children of all races, religions, and even sexual orientations.

No, I am not talking about the children's parents; I am talking about the children themselves. Children today, even young ones, are being encouraged to explore their gender identity, different religious options, and even how they define themselves in terms of race (mixed-race children might identify themselves one way or another or as both). Besides wanting to avoid making mistakes that could land you in sensitivity training or being officially reprimanded, you need to be prepared to treat all of your students equally and not interfere with how the parents are raising their children, no matter what your personal opinion may be.

MISTAKE 154

Letting your religion show…

The percentage of atheists in the U.S. is relatively small, so it is probably safe to conclude that the majority of your students will be people of faith. But we are not all people of the same faith. Even among those who practice the same faith, there are variations on the theme. While I understand that some religions teach their practitioners to live their life as a witness, evangelizing in the classroom is a mistake and could get you fired.

Furthermore, you should go ahead and dismiss any negative ideas you have of other faiths before you come face-to-face with a child being raised in that faith and say something offensive. When you lecture on religious groups in history, be sure to use facts, not opinions. It is a fact to say that a Pope was once so powerful that he was able to order a Crusade into the Holy Lands. It is conjecture to suggest that Catholics once felt justified in killing Jews and Muslims. Even if the latter is reasonably safe to assume based on the truth of the former, it is best for you to present history in terms of facts, and let your students draw their own conclusions.

If you happen to be an atheist, it is equally damaging for you to let any disdain you feel for the religion your students practice show. Debating on matters of faith and whether or not there is a God is best saved for college campuses and coffee houses, not an eighth-grade classroom. No matter what you think of a student's spiritual beliefs, keep it to yourself.

One final note in this area: you should show respect for religious holidays and customs. Children of all religions will be excused from school to observe their holy days. Do not act as if you cannot be bothered to accommodate their schedules or demand the completion of an assignment directly after a religiously excused absence. No matter how annoyed you might feel that every faith's high and holy days cannot be concentrated into spring, winter, and summer breaks, do not allow this annoyance to cause you to commit mistakes in how you treat your students.

MISTAKE 155
Only celebrating "common" holidays...

As a tangent to the issue of religion, do not tell your class you are only going to celebrate "real" holidays, "American" holidays, or anything else like that. While you might just be looking to celebrate the secular Christmas, it would not do you any harm to spend part of a day discussing how so many world religions have special holidays at the same time of year. You can also discuss the different legends that arose around Christmas throughout the world.

Using an approach like this should allow you to experience the holidays with your students without offending any particular group of students in the process.

MISTAKE 156
Letting stereotypes show up in your classroom...

Even when you are teaching young children, you need to make sure you and your students check their stereotypes at the door. Even if the stereotype seems positive, like all Asians are good and math and science, it has no place in your classroom. You are there to teach students who will have varying degrees of talent in science, history, math, language, music, athletics, reading, art, and so on. You need to create an atmosphere where each student can discover where their talent lies and exactly what their strengths and weaknesses will be.

If you approach teaching or allow your students to approach learning from a point of preconceived notions not based on performance, you will limit your children from the start. If you find yourself thinking a student will be good or bad at something based on nothing else but their gender or ethnicity, dismiss that notion completely, and discover if the child is talented in that area or not.

MISTAKE 157
Treating girls and boys differently...

At the time this book was written, professional football players are making headlines for domestic abuse. It is an incredibly embarrassing time as coaches and leaders are figuring out exactly how they will deal with this issue and the behavior of their players. One of the most common things said about this issue is that a man never has a right to hit a woman, no matter what.

Translate this idea to middle or high school students, and you get the message that it is fine for a girl to sock a guy in the mouth, but that same guy is not allowed to do anything to defend himself. If you allow this mentality to seep into your classroom, you will establish the precedent for teens to think that there is one set of rules for girls and another set of rules for boys.

It is as simple as that. The battle of the sexes begins in school as does the simple question — are we equal or not? No matter what your personal opinion on this matter is, legally, you are required to create a classroom atmosphere where the genders are considered equal. Since that is your responsibility, I recommend that you dispense with the old ideas that girls can hit boys, but boys cannot hit girls and other such nonsense. Discipline students equally for equal offenses, and you will send the message clearly to your students that you do not believe girls are better than boys or vice versa.

This is important not just for maintaining your classroom and avoiding sensitivity training, but it is vital to the learning process as well. While the pendulum has certainly been swinging, certain college majors and industries are still predominately thought of as "male" or "female." If you have a girl who is good in science or a boy who is good at art, you do not want old fashion ideas of what girls and boys should be doing to seep into your classroom and poison a child against pursuing an area of natural talent.

The more ways you can communicate equality between the genders, the less likely it will be that your students will come to think of an area of learning to be for "boys" or "girls" only. This will ultimately allow your students the best possible learning environment, and it should be your goal for every class you teach.

MISTAKE 158

Not protecting students who may be gay...

The middle and high school ages are a time when children are becoming sexually self-aware. This means that gay students will transition past the point where they realize they are a bit "different" and become aware of their attraction to the same sex. Of course, recognizing an attraction is a long way away from living and dating as openly gay.

Depending on the societal make up of the area in which you live, your experience with gay students could range from having an active LGBT community to a place that makes being open about your sexuality seem like an impossibility. No matter what your personal opinion in regards to homosexuality or same-sex relationships, for legal reasons, you need to take measures to protect all of your students.

Furthermore, a child can be bullied by being called gay even if they have no such leanings. Make sure that you recognize if a child is being bullied because she is too much of a "tomboy" or because he is too feminine. While girls and boys are different and any endeavor to create a gender neutral world is futile, you should still make sure that children are not being made fun of because of antiquated ideas of what it means to be a boy or girl. Just because a boy is not good at or does not like sports does not mean he is going to grow up to like other boys. And if a girl happens to play video games with her brothers and likes football more than dolls, that is no indication that she will grow up to prefer the company of women. By not allowing your students to perpetuate foolish ideas like these or attach negative feelings to the idea of being gay, you will do a lot to protect the self-esteem of any student in your classroom that may later come out.

MISTAKE 159

Allowing students to make fun of a child's accent or culture...

Some children have a tendency to find anything that is different amusing or tease worthy. A student who has a heavy accent or dresses differently because of her family's culture could be subject to ridicule or scorn. You should do what you can to put a halt to that type of behavior in your classroom and teach respect to all of your students.

MISTAKE 160

Assuming a student needs extra help if they are from another country/culture...

A good friend of mine, Sigmarie Soto, is from Puerto Rico, but grew up in the states. She explains that wrong assumptions hindered her academic advancement early on. "In first grade, I was assigned to a bilingual class because of, what I suppose, was an overflow of students.

Although I am a native Spanish speaker, I learned to speak and read English at home with my mother. Because the students in this class were still learning how to read in English, I was going at a slower pace. For example, when the teacher would put us into a 'reading circle' a few times a week, the allotted time would be over before I even got a chance to read."

If a lack of opportunity to participate was the only thing that came of this situation, it would not be so bad, but Sigmarie goes on to explain, "Close to the end of one of the semesters, my mother received a letter saying that I would fail first grade, and that more specifically, I was failing reading. My mother checked on this, because I read in English at home all of the time, and after talking to the principal and teacher, they had a third party come in and test me and a couple of other students separately. I ended up with above average results on the test, but this could have been avoided if the teacher would have assessed the need and reading level of each student at the beginning of the year instead of making assumptions."

There are many lessons to be learned from Sigmarie's story, but I think of the most vital to this point is that even if you hear a student speaking fluent Spanish (or some other language) in the halls, do not assume they are not fully bilingual and capable of excelling in English. Also, do not allow them to use "English is not my first language" as a crutch. Even if you teach science or history, expecting a student to use proper grammar and spelling on tests and in papers is not unreasonable. You may not want to grade them down as much as an English teacher would, but you can still incorporate these elements into your grading scale.

MISTAKE 161

Not helping children who live in poverty keep up with the class...

Some families can barely afford clothes and shoes to send their children to school. Be aware of your student's financial backgrounds before you send home assignments that require even small purchases. If a student tells you that he or she could not complete an assignment because they did not have the supplies, be sympathetic, and provide them with an alternate opportunity. I know you will not always be able to supply your class on your budget, but be aware that parents have budgets too, and some of them are incredibly tight.

PART FOUR

PROFESSIONAL MISTAKES TO AVOID

As a new teacher, you probably have, at most, a one-year contract. No matter how secure a teacher's position with tenure may be, you could do your job perfectly and still not be renewed the following year. Follow the advice in this section to give yourself the best shot at a more permanent contract.

CHAPTER 21
Choosing Your School Environment

This book would not be complete without at least some words of caution when it comes to selecting the school where you will work. Your first thought might be to accept whatever job comes your way, and you may need to do so in order to get your career started. However, if you do have a choice, keep in mind some of the differences that come with public and private schools.

MISTAKE 162
Not understanding how different types of "public" schools work…

Public schools have come under increased criticism in recent years, but they are still the most prevalent form of education offered in the U.S. If you work in a public school environment, government mandates can impact your curriculum choices, and you may find yourself having to meet a lot of requirements that you do not entirely understand. If you teach in a state with mandatory testing, you may find yourself feeling burdened by having to ensure your students achieve a certain level of test scores.

The charter school is a branch off of the traditional public school in that it is still funded by the government, but it operates without many of the regulations affecting normal public schools. These alternative institutions were first launched in the 1990s, and they can provide a different type of school structure to their students. Generally speaking, charter schools seem to have been proven successful in providing a better education and student experience.

As a teacher at a charter school, you might have fewer students per class, more freedom to design your curriculum, and your job will be tied to the school's success. If the school fails to meet the requirements of their charter, it could close. When you are applying to different schools and eventually accept your first job, be sure you understand the rules and regulations you will be operating under for your first year of teaching.

MISTAKE 163

Not understanding the requirements of various "private" schools…

If your first teaching job is at a private school, you too must understand the unique standards you will be expected to meet. Private schools can vary dramatically in their setup and core beliefs. These can include preparatory schools where parents send their children with the expectation that the school will prepare their children for college, military academies, and religious schools.

Being hired at any one of these schools will come with certain expectations. If you happen to agree with the school's ideology, you will probably fit in just fine. But if you have issues where you disagree with what the school teaches, you will need to decide ahead of time how to deal with that, or you could risk your job.

CHAPTER 22
Behavioral Mistakes

This chapter is dedicated to compiling in one place several mistakes you could make in regards to how you behave on the job. If you can avoid these mistakes, you should be able to prevent any serious issues of discipline or reprimand.

MISTAKE 164
Using language not fit for children to hear…

I dedicated a section to how you should avoid cursing in front of your students, but you should probably avoid inappropriate language at work altogether. While I am sure many teachers will use more adult language in their break room, it is probably best that you try not to flip back and forth between knowing when you can and cannot say certain things.

Note that there are words that might not be considered "curse" words, but they should still be excluded from your vocabulary completely. From racial slurs to gender-specific insults, you probably already know the words and phrases you should avoid. Remember that just like there is appropriate attire for work and "going out" clothes you can wear with your friends, your language needs to follow the same rules. Just because you use a word with your friends and do not think anything of it does not mean you can speak like that at work. When in doubt, err on the side of caution.

MISTAKE 165
Showing prejudice or bias...

Just like any professional environment, you have to comply with certain standards and expectations. One of the biggest ways you could get yourself in trouble is to demonstrate racism, sexism, or any other bias that could be perceived by your students or coworkers.

You should assume there is no "safe" prejudice you can demonstrate in the workplace. We live in a far more diverse world than before, and even the smallest towns may have students who are Muslim, Indian, or are the children of two mommies. No matter what your opinion is on race, religion, gay marriage, or nationality, you should probably make it a point to not make disparaging remarks to your students or coworkers about any minority group.

Furthermore, in your efforts to minimize bullying in your classroom and school, it would be best for you to lead by example and not make jokes at anyone's expense. It can lighten things up to crack a joke once in a while, but keep the jokes neutral and safe. When a child sees you make a joke about someone, they may think it is safe for them to do so. Being careful in this regard will set the right tone for your classroom and will protect you professionally.

> **MISTAKE 166**
>
> ## Not being smart about your social media...
>
> You have been told this countless times — make sure your social media profiles are professional, and do not post anything you would not want your pastor or grandmother to see. However, it is still important that you carefully browse through your posts, your photos, and all of your personal information with the perspective of a future employer.
>
> There may be posts that seem arrogant, photos that you took of an unknowing subject, or an awkward relationship status that you would not want your future boss to see. Take the precaution of checking all of your social media and either make certain things private or delete anything that could give off a bad impression of yourself. And definitely do not let your profile picture be a photo of you flicking off the camera (I have seen this).

MISTAKE 167

Dressing inappropriately...

Your school likely has a dress code for you to adhere to, and there will be scheduled days for casual wear. However, you should likely do more than meet the dress code early in your career. Career coaches have loads of advice to share with candidates on how to dress for interviews. And I have heard of people not getting a job simply because they did not meet a certain standard for interview attire.

It is almost disturbing to think that qualifications can be overlooked if a dress code is not properly met. However, in today's market where there are more qualified candidates than job slots, every bit of distinction can separate one person from another. During your first year, you are in many ways still a job candidate.

Therefore, it will probably serve you well to dress a little nicer than required throughout the school year. There will certainly be times when wearing a school t-shirt and jeans is more than appropriate, but otherwise, dress it up rather than down.

MISTAKE 168
Dating someone on the staff…

Of all the places a single person can meet someone to date, work is the number one location for most. However, dating someone in the workplace is usually frowned upon, even in the corporate environment. At a school, you might have fewer opportunities, but it is an equally bad idea.

If you meet someone at the school, date, and eventually marry, everything could come up roses. However, if you end the relationship at some point, it could create a very awkward work environment for both of you. As a new teacher, you do not need to add stress to an already stressful job. It is for the best that you keep your work and personal life separate, and if possible, date outside of the school.

MISTAKE 169
Dating a parent...

I do not recommend that you start dating the parent of one of your students under any circumstances. There are many reasons why this could be a complicated and needlessly stressful endeavor on your part, not the least of which is how you would relate to the teen's other parent.

If you find yourself growing interested in the parent of one of your students, and you believe they return the interest, the school year goes by quickly. Once the child is out of your classroom, you can try to pursue a relationship at that time, but while you are teaching Tom or Sarah, go ahead and rule their parents out as possible romantic interests. This advice will protect you professionally and will spare you from becoming the subject of the school rumor mill.

MISTAKE 170

Not reporting illegal behavior…

As a teacher in middle school and high school, you will likely witness a slew of bad behavior, ranging from bullying to drug deals. In the roughest of schools, gang members might exercise certain methods to intimidate not only students, but also teachers. You need to take the necessary steps to protect yourself legally. Therefore, if you witness illegal behavior, you need to report it. No matter what threats, bribes, or pleas get levied your way, it is ill-advised to turn a blind eye to behavior that should be brought to the attention of the principal. Failing to do so could make you the subject of a lawsuit and/or could get you fired.

CHAPTER 23
Continuous Improvement

As a teacher, you will be called upon to complete several hours of professional development throughout your career, and you will be expected to continuously work to improve your performance in the classroom. You might as well begin this process in your first year of teaching and perhaps impress your boss in the process.

MISTAKE 171

Not working on your classroom presentation skills...

Hopefully you are an eloquent speaker who does not get tongued-tied or find yourself at a loss for words. However, if you still need to improve your lecture or presentations skills, be sure to practice this as the year goes on. I am certain that you will be observed at times to evaluate your performance. When this happens, you want to make sure you are comfortable leading your classroom and are free of verbal pauses and lapses. Since practice makes perfect, work on this with friends, in front of the mirror, and perhaps even ask a mentor to observe your classroom before your evaluation to provide you tips and recommendations.

MISTAKE 172

Not planning ahead...

In the first chapter, I reviewed how important it is to plan for the first day/week of school, but that is not where the advanced planning ends. You will want to plan weeks in advance for delivering your curriculum, tests, and special projects. You need to take a look at the school calendar and see how to fit your curriculum plan into the school schedule to make things easiest on the students. You do not have to have a plan so firm that you never deviate from it — just make sure you are not "making it up as you go along."

MISTAKE 173

Not adjusting your lesson plan if needed...

If something comes up that you failed to anticipate, make sure you are willing to alter your lesson plan to accommodate needed changes. This could be due to children needing more time on the material or an interesting learning opportunity arose that you want to take advantage of. While it is vital to plan ahead, it is also important to be flexible enough that you can always put educating your students first.

MISTAKE 174

Not adjusting your teaching methods if they appear ineffective...

Since you are new to teaching, it is reasonable that you will need to make changes to your teaching strategies throughout the year. There may be nothing wrong with your approach (in theory), but it could just not be working for you and your students. Whether this is a change in testing strategies or trying a new approach in how you communicate a lesson, be open to trying something new if it will help your students better master the material they need to learn.

MISTAKE 175

Not reviewing what types of questions your students are struggling with...

Every time you give a test, you have an opportunity to evaluate where your students are struggling on an individual level, but also as a group. If you find that most of your students are having a hard time with a specific type of problem, you should spend extra time reviewing that material and practicing how to answer those questions. If all you do is grade the tests and send them home, you miss an opportunity to improve your teaching approach.

CHAPTER 24
Avoiding a Lawsuit

It is almost a shame that I have to include a chapter like this, but it is also easy to get sued in today's world (or at least threatened with one). In order to protect yourself against litigation and disciplinary measures by your administration, avoid the mistakes laid out in this chapter.

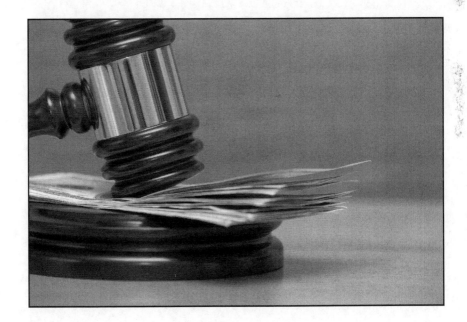

MISTAKE 176

Not knowing applicable laws for schools in your county/state...

Ignorance of the law is not a defense for breaking it. This common axiom is the reason why saying you did not see the speed limit will not save you from a ticket. Breaking the law at your school as a first year teacher will undoubtedly make it difficult for you to advance your career. Make sure you know the laws and regulations that apply to your school, and make every effort to comply with them.

MISTAKE 177

Not making students aware of risks, even ones you think they should know...

As foolish as it may sound, if you fail to make teens aware of potential danger, and they get hurt, you could be considered liable. Therefore, put some thought and consideration into what dangers your students face in your classroom and what safety rules you need to brief your students on. For example, even if you are sure they know not to run with scissors, go ahead and tell them not to all the same.

MISTAKE 178

Not monitoring your students closely while they are in your care...

On a related note, be sure you keep a diligent eye on the students in your class. When they are in your care, if something happens to them, parents will hold you accountable. Be careful about stepping outside, allowing yourself to be distracted for an extended period of time, or focusing too intently on an activity that you lose track of what is going on in your classroom. Even if you allow your students some free time, keep an eye of them to make sure no one is doing something stupid or dangerous.

MISTAKE 179

Purposively embarrassing a student...

I have detailed how being snide, sarcastic, or rude to a child is unprofessional and unlikely to achieve your purpose. However, you should be aware that embarrassing or harassing a student on purpose is also a good way to get yourself reprimanded or named in a lawsuit. If you are ever tempted to speak harshly to a student (no matter how justified it may seem), be cautious, bite your tongue, and keep silent.

MISTAKE 180

Not removing a student who proves dangerous to another student...

You know that you need to maintain a safe, bully-free classroom. If you feel that a student is starting to pose a danger to another child, do not ignore your gut feeling. Send the child to the office, and report the issue to administration. Hopefully, your principal can take the needed steps to get the aggressor in line so that there are no instances of violence. While some old-fashioned parents might not blink an eye at a couple of boys getting into a tussle, many parents today would be very upset if their child was hurt at school. Do not let any such incident happen on your watch.

MISTAKE 181

Not protecting a student's privacy...

In an earlier chapter, I advised against engaging in gossip in regards to your coworkers or student parents. When it comes to your students, do not discuss their private issues needlessly. If you want to seek the advice of a mentor and explain the problem you are facing with a student, try to do so without naming the child. In the instances where it is necessary to discuss the child by name, be sure that you are doing so for the good of the student.

MISTAKE 182
Not complying with laws regarding suspicion you must report...

There are instances where you learn — or think you have learned — information that you are required to report to the appropriate authorities. If you think you are obligated to report something, but are unsure how to do it or who to contact, consult someone at the school who is qualified to advise you; perhaps you can turn to a school psychologist, a mentor teacher, or your principal.

MISTAKE 183
Not knowing your student's medical needs...

Hopefully your students do not have overly complicated medical needs, but if they are facing severe allergies or other potential health risks, you need to be aware of them and know what to do in the case of an emergency. This is doubly true if you are going on a field trip with your class. Do not take it for granted that all of your children are as healthy as a horse — make sure you review their files for any information you need to remember throughout the school year.

MISTAKE 184

Not documenting communications with parents...

On the slight chance a parent takes issue with you and calls you out in front of your boss, be sure that you have documented your communications with the parents well. This could be as simple as keeping track of emails and notes sent home to the parents of all your students. If you take care throughout the school year to document communications with parents, you will not find yourself needing to scramble later in the year if there is an issue. You might also consider creating email folders for your students where you can put any incoming messages from parents. This is quick and easy, and it will make your life easier if something does come up in the future.

MISTAKE 185

Using a student's image without their parents' permission...

This is pretty straightforward — do not use images of your students without permission. Do not post their images in your newsletters or on a social media page. Do not use their image in any way without first getting signed permission from a parent.

MISTAKE 186

Dating a student or former student...

I would love to believe there is no reason for me to include this note, but there are times when the age difference between teacher and student is going to be very small. A senior in high school can be as old as 18 or 19, and therefore, technically legal to date. Even if your school district does not list this as grounds for firing, I still strongly recommend against such entanglements.

Furthermore, I strongly recommend that you do not date a former student in close proximity to their graduation. I realize that a student can come home from on break during their freshmen year of college, be 18 or 19 years old, and seem appealing to a 23 year old former teacher. While this might technically be acceptable, it could paint you in an undesirable light.

First, suspicion that you were dating the student when they were still in school could arise. Second, if they have friends who are still in school, possibly in your class, this could lead to issues with fraternization and appearing to be their peer rather than their teacher. While you might not get sued or fired for this practice, it is still not the best career decision you could make.

MISTAKE 187

Drinking or smoking at school...

There will likely be a designated smoking area at your school for the teachers. In many states, it will be outside because of laws regarding smoking in work environments or public facilities. While it is permissible to go outside and smoke during your breaks, if you can avoid it, you might want to consider doing so.

The anti-drug use movement in schools is pretty strong these days. If a student sees you smoking, it could remove a certain amount of the respect they hold for you. Until they become jaded, students expect teachers to represent all the instructions that are being imparted on them. Therefore, if you tell your students not to smoke, you should practice that policy yourself even though you are old enough, and they are not.

The recommendation not to drink at work should be a "no-brainer," as they say. However, there was at least one teacher at my high school that was rumored to have a flask in her desk, and her breath reportedly smelled of liquor throughout the day. Do not put yourself in that situation, as it would undoubtedly cost you your job.

MISTAKE 188

Showing physical displays of affection with students or a teacher…

No matter what age of student you are teaching, physical displays of affection or comfort need to be done cautiously and sparingly. The same rule applies to your teachers and coworkers. I do not want to believe we live in an age where you cannot hug a student or coworker who tells you that there has been a death in their family or some other upsetting news. You do need to be ever cautious of the risk of being accused of sexual harassment. What seems innocent to you could be perceived as unwelcome physical contact to someone else. The best policy is probably a complete hands-off approach; otherwise, my best advice is to proceed with extreme caution — not everyone is a "hugger."

CHAPTER 25
Impressing Office Staff/Your Boss

You never get a second chance to make a good first impression. Over the course of your first year of teaching, you want to make every effort to put your best foot forward. That is why you should be extra cautious to act in a professional manner at all times. In order to establish a good relationship with the office staff (who can make your life so much easier) and your boss, avoid the mistakes listed in this chapter.

MISTAKE 189
Avoiding extra work…

The teachers who were interviewed for this book have stated things such as, *"Do not get involved in campus politics,"* or *"Do not get burned out."* However, you still need to be "true to your school," so to speak. You cannot dodge school events, even if somehow they do not involve you or your students. You cannot avoid all PTA activities, fundraisers, and other activities and expect to be viewed positively by your employer.

While you do not need to volunteer or work yourself into the ground, it is smart to attend social events, eat lunch with your colleagues, and stop for small talk now and then. Additionally, if you can help a teacher out from time to time, you will find it easier to ask them for help if you ever need it. You are part of a team and need to prove yourself to be a valuable member.

MISTAKE 190

Not being considerate when using copiers and office equipment...

You are going to need to make copies, send faxes, and use other front-office equipment as much as any other teacher. Just be sure that you are considerate while doing so. Follow whatever rules and procedures your school has for use of office equipment, and pay attention to other people who may be waiting in line for use of equipment. If you have a lot of copies to make, let someone with a short stack move ahead of you, and try not to ask any of the office staff to move a huge stack of work for you.

MISTAKE 191
Being overly defensive if a parent or student complains about you…

If a parent or student does file a complaint about you, defend yourself through documentation, and approach the situation in a professional manner. Being overly defensive, argumentative, or emotional when speaking to your boss about an accusation against you will not help your case. Remain calm and reasonable, and you can get your boss on your side, defending you to the parent or student. Any other approach and you might find yourself facing off against both the parent and administration.

MISTAKE 192
Taking too many sick days…

As you make every effort to create a good impression with your boss, you should know that taking too many days off will not accomplish this goal. While sick days cannot be helped, do not take days off without good cause. You do not want to go to school and give an entire class of children a bad case of the flu, of course, but work hard to maintain good health (get a flu shot, take your vitamins, etc.).

MISTAKE 193
Going over someone's head...

Whether you by-pass someone by making a simple maintenance request or purposively skip over someone you know is in your chain-of-command, there is not much you can do that will ruffle someone's feathers more than going over their head. While the situation may come up where this is necessary, do so with great caution.

MISTAKE 194
Complaining about the classes you are assigned to teach...

New teachers will often be assigned to the least desirable classes. If this conflicts with your idea of instructing the next generation of business leaders and scientists, do not make your dissatisfaction known. Even if you feel you are the best qualified to teach more advanced classes, you might still need to work your way into those roles. After all, teaching students who want to go to college is often more pleasurable than teaching those who will barely be able to graduate, but they are equally important. Do your best in whatever classes you are assigned to lead, and eventually, you will receive the more ideal courses.

CHAPTER 26
Final Thoughts

A great deal of this book has been dedicated to flooding you with awful mistakes you can make in your first year of teaching that could leave a bad impression on your students, their parents, or your colleagues. I do not want to conclude this book without reminding you that your job does not have to be miserable or nothing but stress. You can have fun as a teacher, and in the end, I hope you find it to be a highly fulfilling profession. Consider these final "mistakes to avoid" to make sure you still find some joy in what you do.

MISTAKE 195

Not smiling…

Do not forget to smile. Even if you are having a bad day, try to remember to smile at your students. When you see them smile back, it will lift your spirits and improve your mood. Plus, as much as you want to be firm, perhaps even strict, with your students in terms of rules and classroom policies, that does not mean that you need to appear to be in a sour mood all of the time. Go ahead and let them see you smile; it will do you and them good.

MISTAKE 196

Not praising a job well done...

Do not be so focused on trying to raise skill levels and overcome areas of weakness that you forget to praise a job well done. Children respond well to praise. They eat it up. You should hand it out generously, but only for positive achievements. You can elect to praise them privately, publically, or both. Just make sure you hand out praise to all of your students. If you look hard enough, you will find a reason to praise even the most difficult student, which could lay the groundwork to turning that relationship around. Additionally, if you do praise children well, it should make it easier in those instances when they need to receive correction from you.

MISTAKE 197

Not being warm and friendly...

While it is important to remain professional with your students, do not feel like you need to maintain a distant, aloof, or cold demeanor. Let yourself be warm and friendly with your students, and you will probably have an easier time teaching them. You want them to feel comfortable approaching you with questions or asking for help, as that will help you get better results. If you act distant, they might not come to you. Find a way to be friendly and kind while maintaining appropriate levels of professionalism and classroom management, and you will set yourself up for a successful first year.

MISTAKE 198
Not making friends among your coworkers...

You do want to avoid school politics, gossip, and drama, but there is no reason why you cannot make friends among your colleagues. If things work out, you will be working with these people for years to come, and you should have a friendly relationship with them. While you want to keep your personal problems away from work, do not be afraid to consider yourself friends with your coworkers. Working in a school is the same as working in any corporate environment — enjoy the company of your colleagues, but remain professional at all work-related events.

MISTAKE 199
Not having any fun...

As strange as it might sound, failing to have any fun during your first year of teaching would be a terrible mistake. You will burn out and probably not want to return for another year whether you get an offer or not. Like I said in the introduction, teaching is one of the most difficult professions to work in — if you cannot enjoy it, you should not be doing it.

BIBLIOGRAPHY

Burruss, Jill D. and Kaenzig, Lisa. "Introversion: The Often Forgotten Factor Impacting the Gifted," Virginia Association for the Gifted Newsletter. 1999 Fall 21 (1).

Hancock, LynNell. "Across the United States, Parents, Teachers, and Administrators Alike are Rethinking Their Approach to After-School Assignments," Smithsonian.com. 2011.

Mason, D.A. & Good, T.L. "Effects of Two-Group and Whole-Class Teaching on Regrouped Elementary Students' Mathematics Achievement," *American Educational Research Journal*. Vol. 30, pp. 328-360. 1993.

Orange, Carolyn. "25 Biggest Mistakes Teachers Make and How to Avoid Them, 2nd Ed." Corwin Press, Thousand Oaks, CA. 2008.

Quercia, Jacopo della. "6 Bizarre Factors That Predict Every Presidential Election," www.cracked.com. (2012).

Silverman, Linda. "What We Have Learned About Gifted Children," www.gifteddevelopment.com. (2014).

Stein, Nathaniel. "Leaded! Harvard's Grading Rubric," *The New York Times*. December 14, 2013.

Strauss, Valerie. "Harvard College's Median Grade is an A-, Dean Admits," *The Washington Post*. December 4, 2013.

CONTRIBUTORS

Bill Hayes
Retired Teacher & Department Head, Leesburg High School

Brandy Lohsl Linville
Former Substitute Teacher/ VPK Teacher, Strawberry Patch Preschool

Brandy Mayer
Clerk of Courts, New Orleans

Christian Langley
Former Teacher/Current Stay-at-Home Dad

Hollis Townsend
Director of Technology Support & Operations
Young Harris College

Jenna Rew
Writing Teacher at Gateway Science Academy High School

Lisa Mikolajczyk
Special Education Teacher

Michael Grigsby
Senior Fiber Engineer
General Dynamics

Peggy Nix
Training & Staffing Solutions Manager
ABTSolutions

Sara Razaire
Volusia County Schools

Shay-Anne Matthews
Former Teacher, Tavares Christian School

Stephen Klubock
Career Coach and Account Manager

Victoria Andrew
Writer/Teacher

INDEX

Absence policy: 7, 76
ADHD: 42, 83, 202, 224
Adjunct: 25
Administration: 13, 25, 29, 35, 116, 230, 261, 264, 273
Affection: 16, 114, 269
After-school help: 134, 176, 223
Assignment: 37, 38, 97, 98, 107, 109, 140-142, 151, 152, 157, 158, 173, 188, 189, 192, 210, 238, 244
Assumption: 149
Attitude: 192
Autocrat: 26
Avoiding inconsistencies: 6, 58, 63

Bathroom breaks: 6, 57
Behavioral issues: 13, 216, 218, 227
Behavioral system: 65, 74
Benjamin Franklin: 35
Bias: 14, 33, 40, 90, 208, 230, 252
Bickering: 7, 88, 229
Biography: 16

Bomb threats: 8, 95, 96
Book reports: 10, 135, 155-157
Bored students: 9, 117, 123
Boundaries: 33, 51, 56
Bullying: 7, 62, 65, 73, 77, 83, 84, 86, 87, 90, 91, 189, 199, 252, 256
Busy work: 9, 98, 136-138

Calendar: 258
Campus politics: 14, 91, 234, 235, 271
Chain-of-command: 274
Cheating: 10, 121, 148-150, 154
Class clown: 6, 47, 50, 53
Classroom control: 7, 66, 77
Classroom policies: 276
Classroom presentation: 15, 257
Common ground: 195
Communication: 94, 127, 128, 197, 216, 219, 220
Complaining: 16, 61, 274
Complex tests: 10, 147
Core subjects: 10, 139, 157
Critical thinking: 127, 128
Criticism: 8, 107-109, 137, 247

Crying: 12, 188-190
Culture: 14, 29, 46, 199, 242, 243
Curriculum planning: 35
Cursing: 7, 70, 71, 137, 251
Curve: 10, 145, 146, 179, 180
Cutting comments: 64

Dating: 15, 21, 241, 254, 255, 267
Defensive: 16, 109, 273
Disability: 12, 13, 115, 201-205, 223
Disciplinary action: 66
Disdain: 62, 225, 237, 238
Disrespectful student: 6, 54, 55
Disruption: 7, 65, 77, 79, 221
Distractions: 7, 20, 83, 84, 91, 95, 101, 136
Divorce: 12, 190, 208, 209, 226-228
Dress code: 32, 253, 254
Drinking: 16, 268
Dyslexia: 42, 203, 224

Emergency: 95, 97, 101, 265
Equipment: 16, 167, 272
Extra credit: 11, 146, 173, 174, 179, 181, 210
Extra work: 7, 16, 79, 80, 173, 174, 271
Extrovert: 12, 196

Failure: 138, 145, 169, 180, 181
Fair testing: 10, 143
False allegation: 14, 236
Familiarity: 30

Family: 13, 141, 157, 226, 227, 230, 231, 242, 269
Favoritism: 6, 13, 60-62, 81, 86, 90, 112, 124, 174, 210, 231, 237
Feedback: 108
Fights: 7, 88, 125
Fire drill: 8, 96
First impression: 271
Flirting: 8, 113, 114
Focus: 28, 36, 50, 74, 90, 114, 121, 123, 169, 182, 208, 226
Fraternizing: 5, 33
Friendly: 16, 276, 277
Friendship: 7, 63, 89, 195
Fun: 5, 12, 14, 16, 18, 36, 68, 69, 79, 99, 120, 152, 156, 157, 185, 186, 191, 242, 275, 277

Gay: 14, 198, 241, 242, 252
Gender: 46, 54, 62, 204, 237, 240, 242
Gifted: 6, 48, 50, 58, 124, 133, 151, 152, 196, 279
Good behavior: 7, 78, 81
Gossip: 14, 208, 235, 236, 264, 277
Grade inflation: 169
Grading scale: 146, 170, 171, 244
Group punishment: 7, 78, 79
Guidance: 14, 21, 104, 113, 164, 190, 213, 219, 224, 233, 234

Hands-on work: 8, 99
Handwriting: 11, 168, 172
History: 11, 101, 104, 123, 158, 160, 167, 170, 183, 195, 202,

238, 239, 244
Holidays: 14, 143, 238, 239
Homework: 9, 10, 37, 62, 69, 75, 79, 80, 99, 103, 107, 119, 135-143, 168, 172, 183, 207, 216, 222, 229

Illegal behavior: 15, 256
Insult: 55, 187
Introvert: 12, 163, 196

Katie Hurley: 63

Lawsuit: 15, 42, 256, 261, 263
Learning disability: 12, 13, 115, 201-205, 223
Learning Environment: 30, 89, 114, 182, 241
Lesson plan: 15, 35, 48, 57, 60, 74, 95, 101, 135, 258
Leveraging: 11, 176, 178
LGBT: 242

Math tests: 11, 165
Medical needs: 15, 265
Memorization: 11, 167
Misunderstanding: 64, 191

Napoleon complex: 55, 56
Neatness: 11, 171, 172

Office equipment: 16, 272
Outside influence: 12, 201
Overcompensating: 6, 55

Paperwork: 37, 41, 227
Parent-teacher conferences: 13, 218
Participation: 11, 49, 124, 135, 170
Personal attack: 12, 109, 187
Personal lives: 12, 208, 235
Personalities: 6, 12, 45, 46, 48, 50, 51, 189, 197
Phone: 84, 112
Plagiarism: 10, 153, 154
Political beliefs: 12, 198
Politics: 14, 22, 91, 234, 235, 271, 277
Popularity: 7, 50, 83, 85, 86
Poverty: 14, 244
Prejudice: 14, 199, 252
Presentation skills: 15, 257
Privacy: 15, 229, 264
Private schools: 14, 247, 248
Professionalism: 5, 29, 33, 47, 53, 56, 61, 62, 70, 71, 228, 276
Psychotherapist: 63
Puberty: 8, 46, 111, 113

Quirk: 198
Quiz: 38, 39, 150

Racism: 61, 199, 252
Re-teaching: 9, 129
Religion: 14, 62, 237-239, 252
Reputation: 49, 63, 67, 123, 235, 236
Respectful: 87
Reward: 7, 78, 81, 99
Ridicule: 6, 66, 68, 69, 242
Rules: 7, 11, 36-39, 51, 58, 59, 65, 92, 94, 120, 121, 127, 130, 138, 165, 167, 168, 179, 193,

203, 240, 248, 251, 262, 272, 275
Sarcasm: 6, 51, 63
Schedule: 8, 10, 76, 101, 103, 105, 113, 131, 136, 139, 140, 142, 143, 150, 176, 209, 218, 227, 258
School breaks: 9, 131
School counselor: 13, 207, 210, 212, 213
School politics: 22, 277
Science projects: 10, 160, 222
Security: 149
Sexual harassment: 8, 113, 236, 269
Sick days: 16, 233, 273
Situational timing: 53
Slang: 5, 32, 33
Smile: 53, 108, 114, 193, 275, 276
Smiling: 16, 275
Smoking: 16, 268
Social media: 14, 32, 253, 266
Special Needs: 6, 42
Spelling rules: 11, 168
Standardized tests: 9, 18, 117, 118, 121, 137, 144, 176
Step-parent: 13, 229
Stereotype: 239
Stereotypes: 14, 54, 239
Stress: 12, 105, 121, 161, 210, 255, 275
Structure: 53, 84, 176, 196, 248
Structure: 53, 84, 176, 196, 248
Student equality: 47
Student handbook: 5, 39
Student orientation: 6, 40

Tablet: 84
Tardy: 7, 57, 75, 76
Teacher's pet: 78, 124
Teaching plan: 205
Teaching style: 59, 60
Teasing: 7, 68, 84-87, 113, 189
Tenure: 22, 245
Textbooks: 100
Transfer students: 9, 132
Tutor: 229

Visual aids: 128, 130
Vomiting: 8, 96

Weaknesses: 6, 43, 56, 118, 133, 134, 177, 219, 240
Well-liked: 185

Yelling: 7, 70-72

AUTHOR BIOGRAPHY

Kimberly Sarmiento is a writer, researcher, and educator who currently leverages a background as a college professor and journalist to provide readers with advice on teaching, career management, and self-marketing. As an instructor, she developed and led undergraduate courses such as *American Federal Government* and *Political Parties and Interest Groups* at Cameron University.

Ms. Sarmiento is a graduate from the University of Florida with a Masters in Political Science and a Bachelors in Journalism. Over the course of her career, she has written for three regional newspapers, authored two books and several blogs on career management, and worked with hundreds of clients on the development of customized résumés and cover letters.

Recently, Ms. Sarmiento has been engaged on a volunteer basis to provide advice to teens on how they can translate high school experience into résumés content for the job market or college admissions. In her spare time, she enjoys going to theme parks with her children and reading.